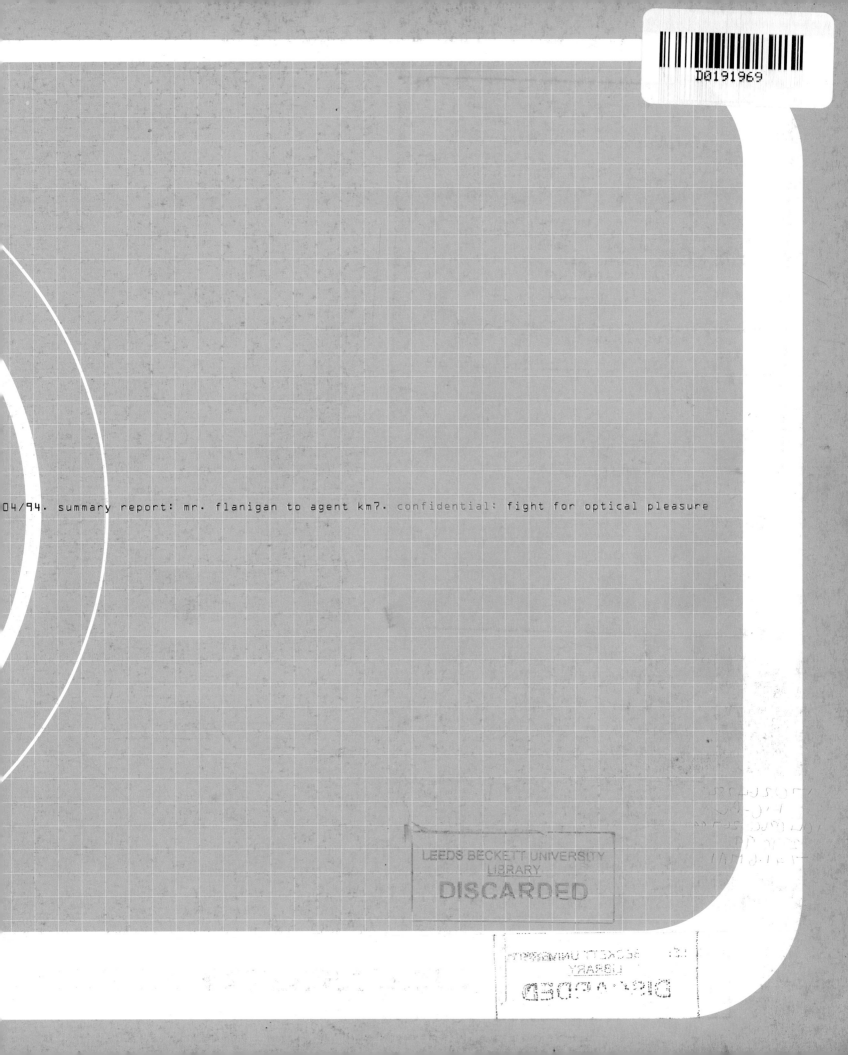

04/94. summary report: mr. flanigan to agent km7. confidential: fight for optical pleasure

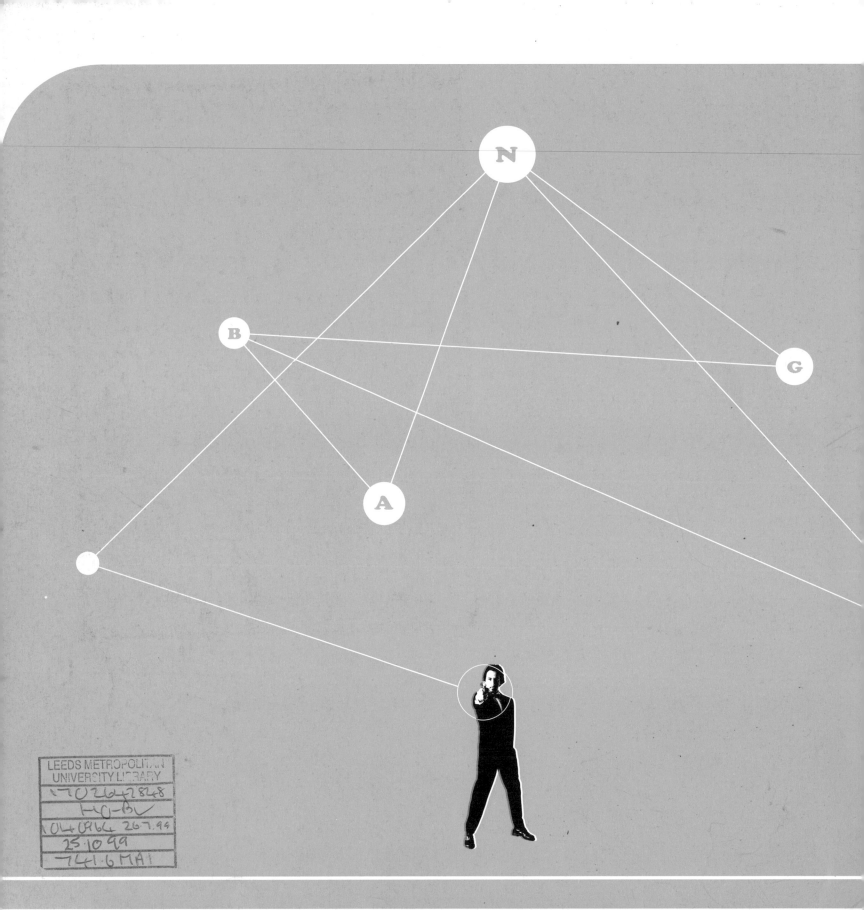

Die Deutsche Bibliothek- CIP Einheitsaufnahme

Mai, Klaus:

Designagent **km7** : Licence To Design / Hrsg.:

Robert Klanten.-

Berlin: Die Gestalten Verlag., 1997

ISBN 3-931126- 14- 5

Designagent **km7** : Licence To Design by Klaus Mai

text by **Louis A. Flanigan** (are u ready)

edited by Robert Klanten

printed by Medialis Offset, Berlin | **Made in Europe**

dgv- Die Gestalten Verlag, Berlin

fax: +49/ 30/30871068 | email: gestalten@contrib.com

designbureau **km7**

schifferstrasse 22, D-60594 frankfurt

phone ++49-69-96 21 81 -30 **fax**

e-mail Klaus.Mai@frankfurt.netsurf

http://www.km7.com

FIGHT FOR OPTICAL PLEASURE

Designagent KM7....
his name is Mai, Klaus Mai and he's on a mission to design a better world. little is known about KM7's early years other than a few facts. born and raised in a small German town, he was restless and set off in search of adventure. his quest took him to all parts of Europe as well as N.Y.C. before finally establishing a base in Frankfurt. while under the guise of his alter ego, Klaus Mai, KM7 was associated with an advertising agency with the suspicious name of Trust.
Trust remained his cover for three long years up until KM7 made his true identity known. For a period of four years KM7 completed mission upon successful mission.

his mark was first made by creating promotions for a then new Frankfurt club, XS.
very quickly his designs caught the eye of chart smashers Jam & Spoon, which led to several chart topping cover designs. along the way his talents have been acquired by Swatch, Nike and Volkswagen.

this book represents KM7's private files and notes on many of his high-profile missions, made public for the first time.

throughout these pages you will find what it takes to have a **Licence to Design.**

Visual translator

OF DA' BASS & DA' BEAT

...uted in the USA and Canada through

...ortium BSD

Westgate Drive

...ul Minnesota 55114/ 1065

12/ 2210124

Distributed in the UK, South America & Asia through

Art Books International

1 Stewart's Court

220 Stewart's Road

London SW 8 4UD   **Great Britain**

fax: 0171/ 7203158

Photos: **Sven Leykauf**

Photos Mission Yello: **Serge Hölschi**

WELCOME

14:02:97 14:33

1 sven**leykauf** (photographer) **2** louis**flanigan** (communicato

9 frank**wuttke** (support) **10** annette**apel** (desig

8 jens**deusner** (media designer)

7 klaus**mai** (designagent)

frankfurt **B** 50°7' **L** 8°40'

7 8 9 10 11 12

hristian**bitenc**(illustrator) **4**andreas**matzke**(3-d) **5**tilman**bares**(graphic designer) **6**sabine**raab**(graphics)

werner**wagner**(musician) **12**volker**stengele**(architect)

THE USUAL SUSPECTS

THEMISSIONS

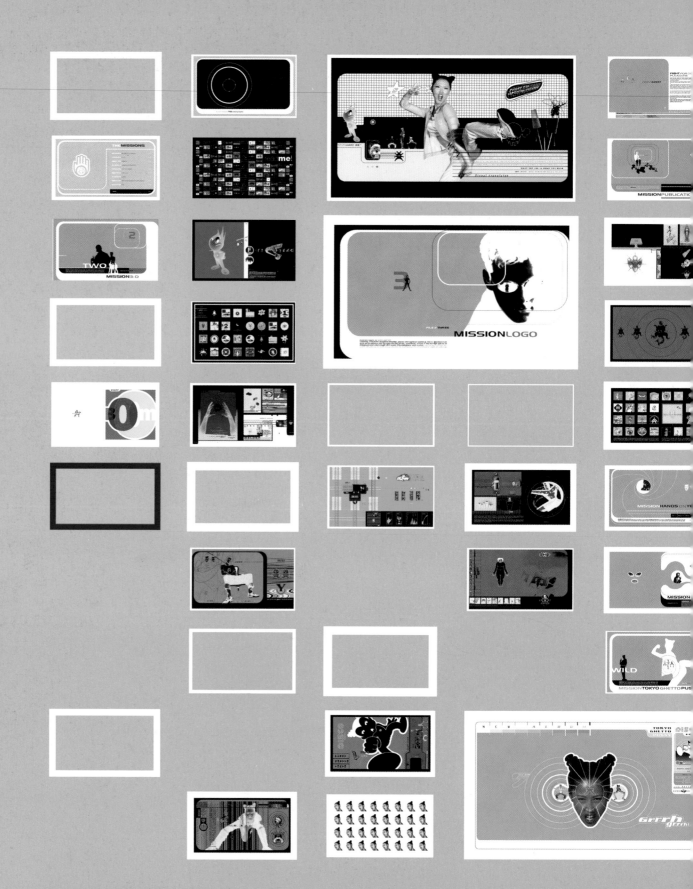

10/11

read**me**!

FILE#ONE

MISSION

"magazine. oh I do so love magazines. **such a simple format, type and image, a marriage made in heave.**
I rarely get a case requiring these special skills. of course when fate presents the mag I take the challenge. probably wh
is most attractive about taking on this type of project for me is breaking the grid. of course having a good content make
the finished results that much better.

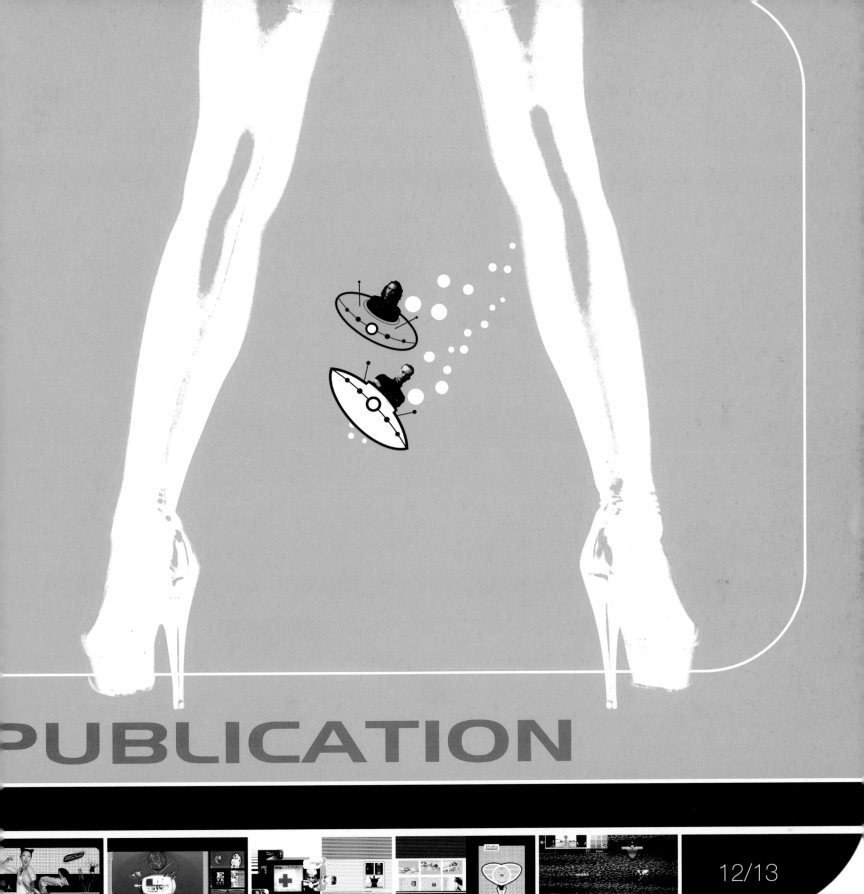

PUBLICATION

12/13

reaking down the grids that bind us all

FIGHT FOR OPTICAL PLEASURE

DESIGN IS A MARRIAGE OF TYPE AND IMAGE. COLOR SPACE AND DIMENSION BECOME GRAPHICS. SOUND AND WORDS MAKE MUSIC. TYPE IS A TOOL AND LINES ARE JUST WEAPONS IN THE FIGHT FOR OPTICAL PLEASURE. IF YOU CAN'T HEAR IT BUT YOU CAN SEE IT, THEN YOU ALREADY FELT IT. MUSIC MOVES AND INDIVIDUAL TO MOTION THROUGH VIBRATION. GRAPHIC DESIGN SHOULD BRING FORTH EMOTION THROUGH VISUALIZATION. DESIGN SHOULD NEVER BE THE SAME:

WHAT YOU SEE IS WHAT YOU HEAR

KM7: VISUAL TRANSLATOR OF DA' BASS & DA' BEAT

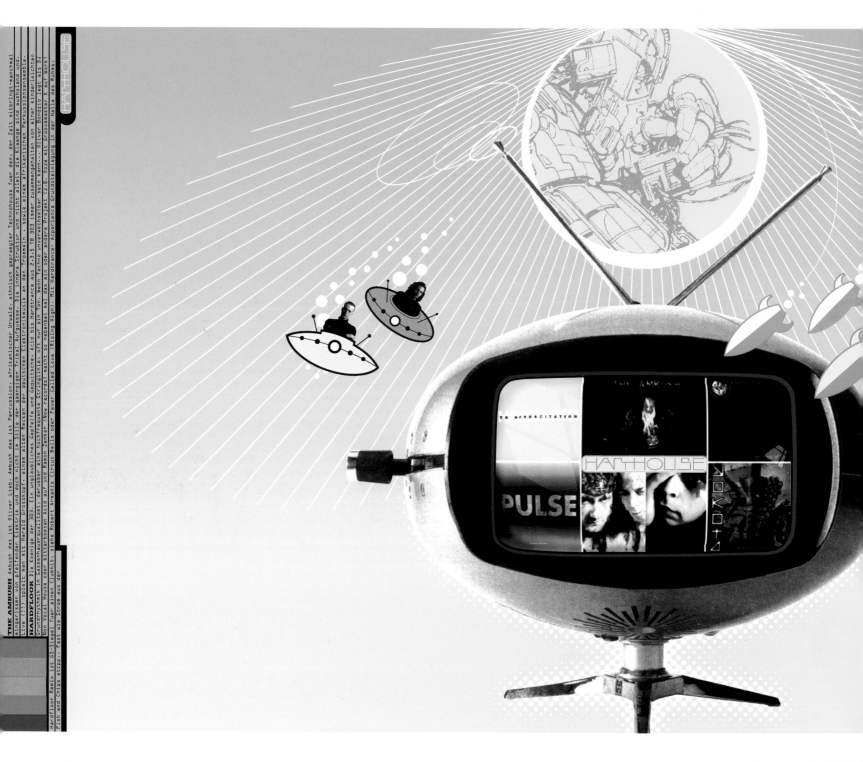

THE AMBUSH Ambush das ist Oliver Lieb. Ambush das ist Percussion, afrikanischer Urwald, ethnisch gepraegter Technohouse fuer den, der Zeit mitbringt-manchmal eingerissen von pfeifender Elektrik und doch nicht im Stile der gaengigen Tribal Aufguesse. Die innere Struktur und nicht allein die Klaenge sind ausholend und.

HARDFLOOR Die Koenige der 303. Ein unglaubliches Gepfeife und Gequitsche. Acid bis Hardtrance aus 2-3-5 TB 303 immer zusammengehalten von einer kinderleichten Grundrhythmik in Gassenhauerqualitaet. darueber eine hochfrequente Stringlinie. oft nur ein Ton. Wenn Techno unverwechselbar sein kann... Oliver Bondzio legt als DJ Non Vocal House oder bitterboesen Acid auf und Ramon Zenker (Now records) macht so nebenbei mal das ein oder andere Projekt (z.B. Ooze mit Groovemaster K auf Work) Hardfloor Remix ist GS-Siegel fuer einen Clubhit: siehe Robert Armanis Circus Bells oder Fever Called Love (Rising High). Mit Hardtrance- Acperience Grundsteinlegung in der Halle des Ruhms. Fish and Chips etcpp- Fast wie Strom aus der

Live (!) spielt man mit Harald Grosskopf, einem alten Recken der deutschen Elektronikmusik an den Trommeln , sowie einem afrikanischen Perkussionsensemble-

age 14+15) **Timing Zero:** graphic design book "visual translator of the da bass and da beat" was the title of this bio piece requested by
e Books of Tokyo. it's hard to do self-promotion, but this was a good opportunity and actually led to the design concept of this book.

age 16+17) **Localizer** was to be the first book representing German designers as well as Germany's much hyped music and club scene.
ges were made to introduce record labels, nightclubs, fashion houses and designers to the general public. in addition to delivering a spread
 KM7, I also designed several companies spreads. among these companies were **Apollo Brand, Groopie, Harthouse** and **Eye Q
ecords. Recycle or die**, shown on the next page, is a sub-label of Eye Q Records which releases ambient tracks from various producers.
ad very little direction and contact with the respective companies and I'm not sure if they even liked the work.

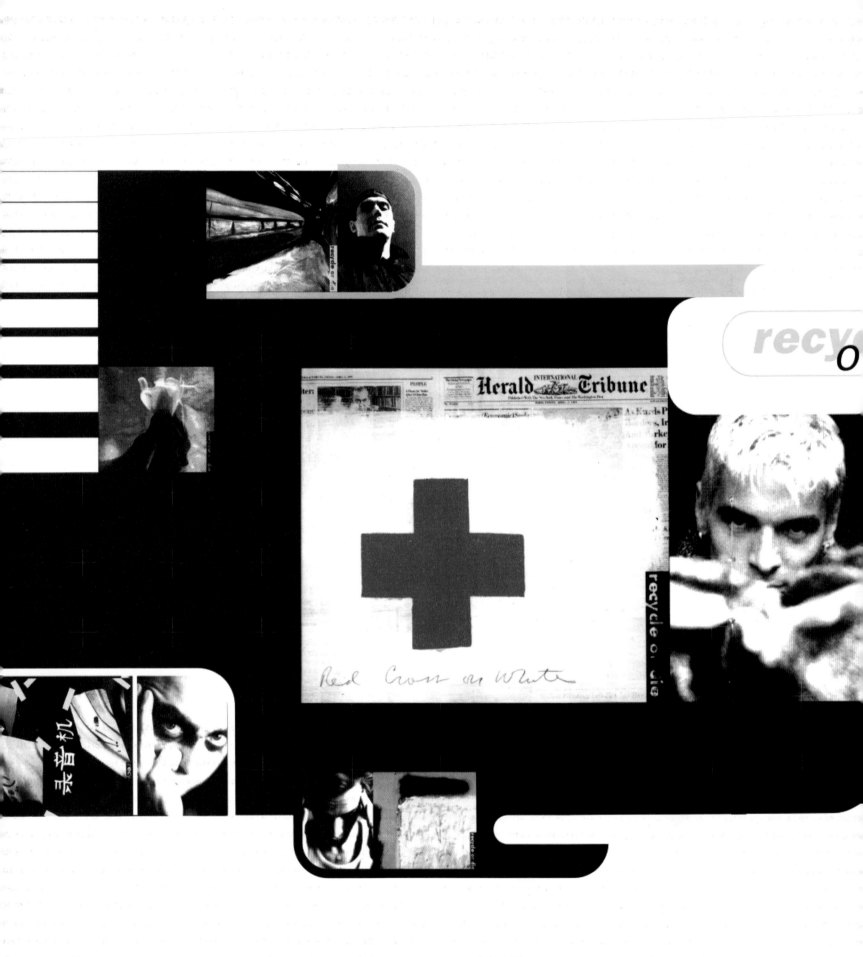

ie

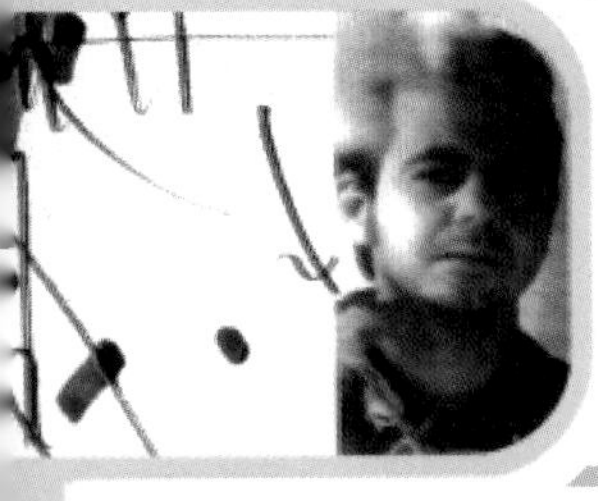

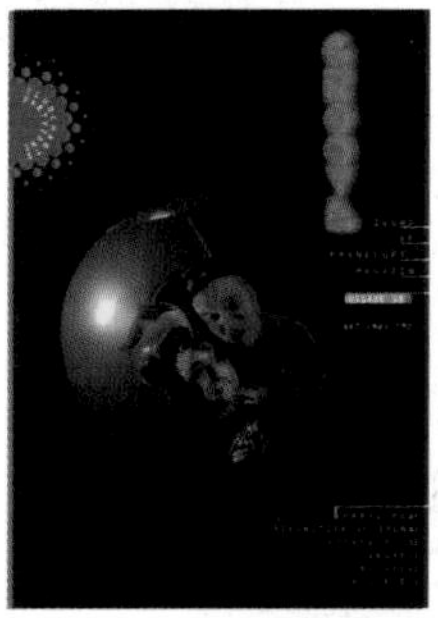

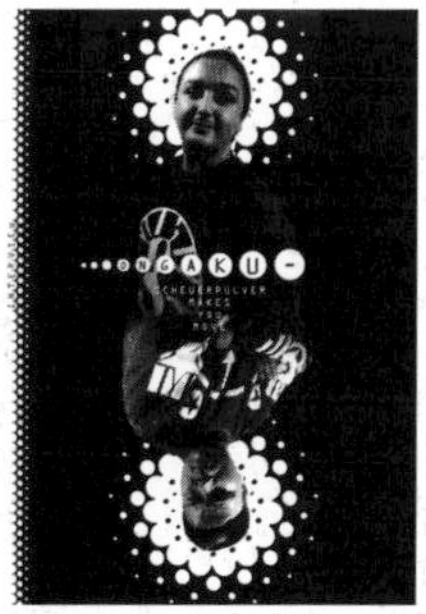

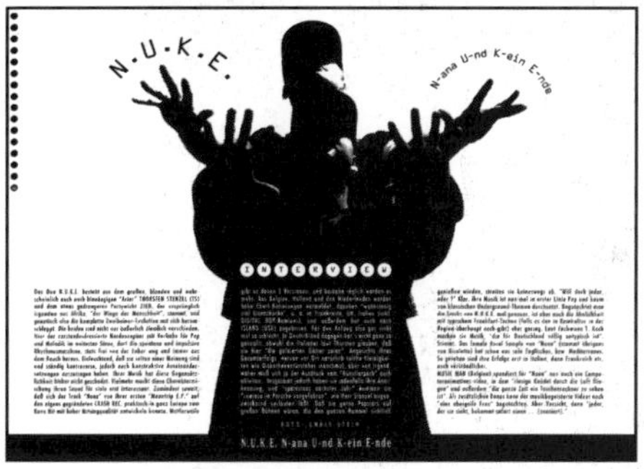

(page 19) Groove Magazine is Germany's oldest music/club culture magazine. when I was approached to design issue 18 I jumped at th chance of doing something radical. with hindsight I put too much time into the basic design and probably took it all too seriously. the result was w accepted and I was asked to continue as art director. but after receiving my bill it was decided the cost of good design was a bit too high.

(page 20) A few spreads taken from a client sponsored magazine, **Instant**. The first was in conjunction with the International ATP Tennis To and the second promoting award-winning industrial design. I completed both magazines while serving time at Trust.

(page 21) Etapes, a French culture magazine, approached me to design their cover. I was free to use any style I desired, but there wa just one thing that I had to put on the cover, besides the logo. it had been a tradition that every cover have on it the letter e. since one of th underlying elements of **"new techno"** is a sense of family and belonging I used a heart to represent love. the "e" element was the easy pa the other side of techno, for a time was a little pill called Ecstasy. "the love drug called techno is all in your head" summed up my feelings this movement and the folks at Etapes agreed.

(page 22+23) In the fall of '96 I was asked by, Frankfurt icon, **Stephan Galloway** to create the design for his new magazine, Slave the Empire. with Galloway's connection to the theater and nightlife culture they planned to publish a mag of interviews, fashion and culture built up the magazine using a line from an older Pet Shop Boys track, Parinio, "...passion love, sex and money". I really was into doing th project, unfortunately Galloway's team never got past the planning stage.

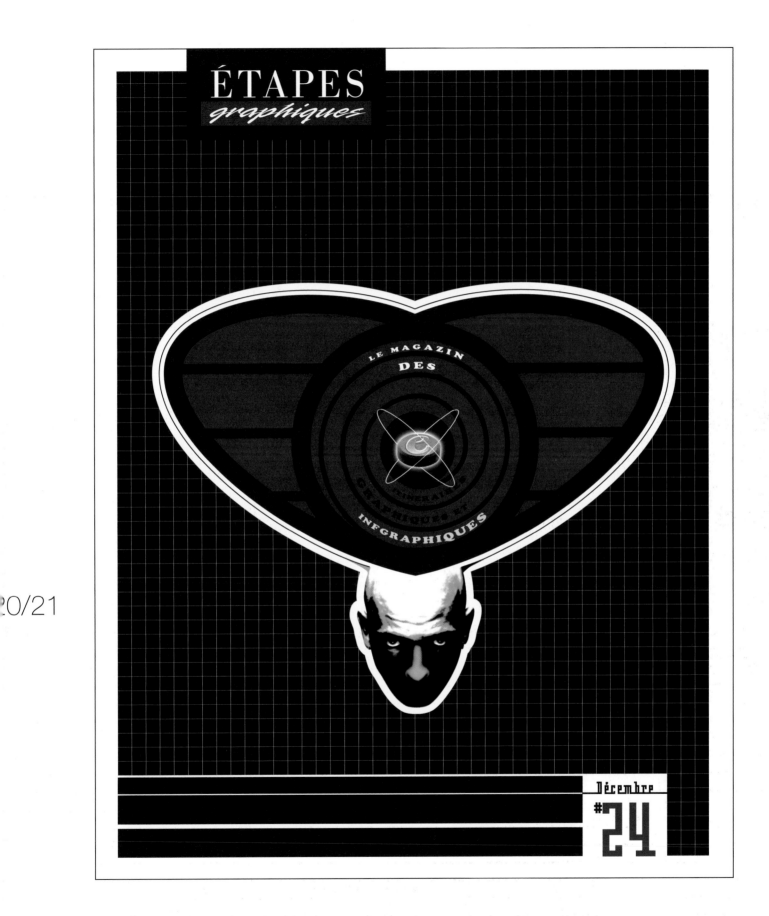

ÉTAPES
graphiques

LE MAGAZIN
DES

INFGRAPHIQUES

Décembre
#24

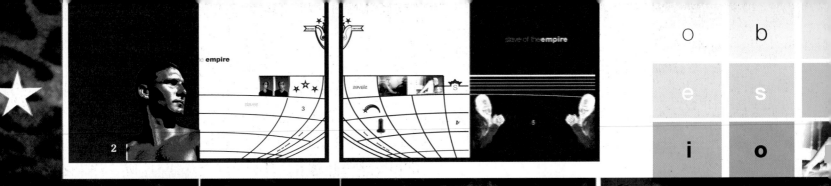

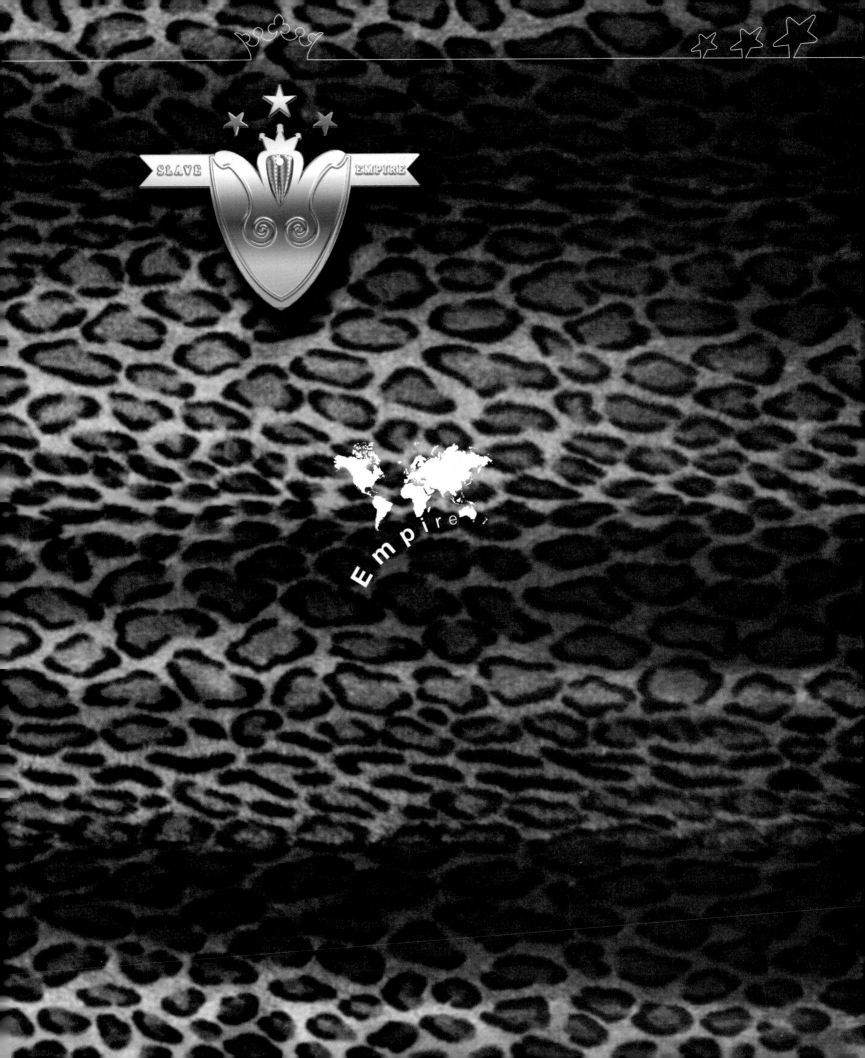

MISSION

TWO

taking design to another plane of exsistence
when computer-generated **3-D images** became all the rave in Europe I did my best to avoid the trend. I always foun
that most of the designs focused too much on the dimensionally enhanced image instead of actually delivering a message
in 1993 3-D imaging was very expensive and took days to complete. in contrast, today there are several good program
for the Mac that make rendering these images cost efficient and quick.

2

FILE#TWO

MISSION3-D

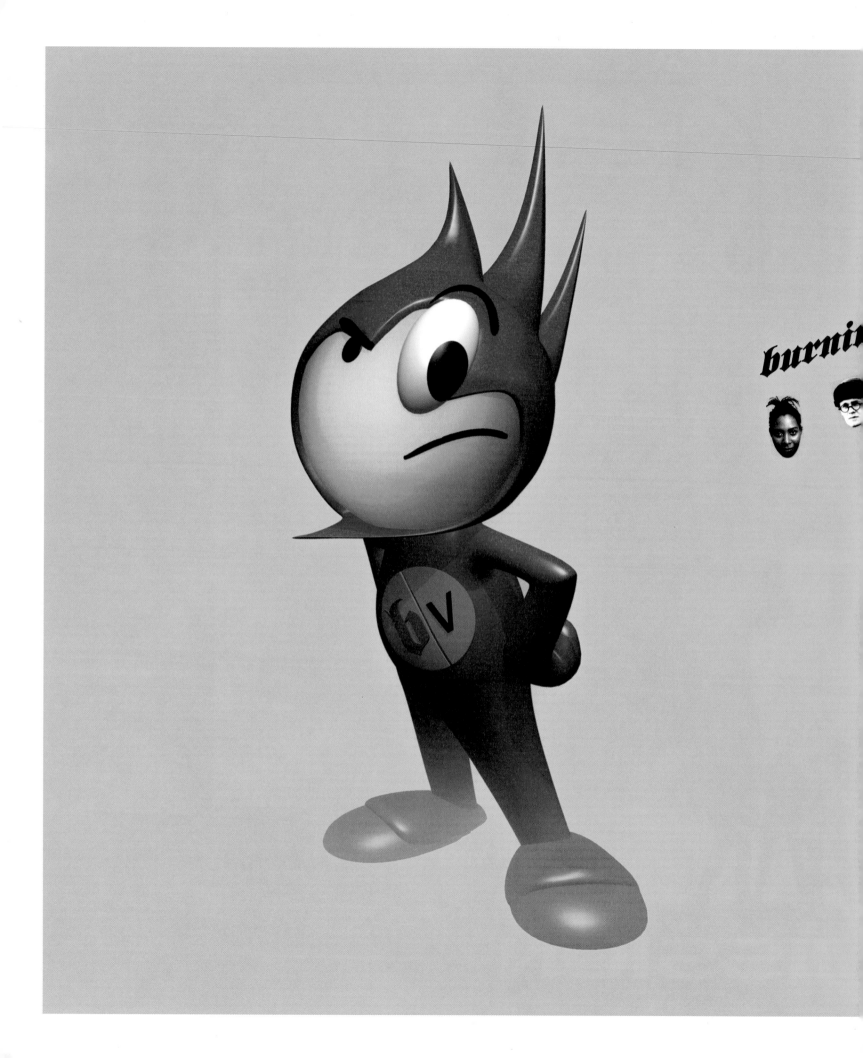

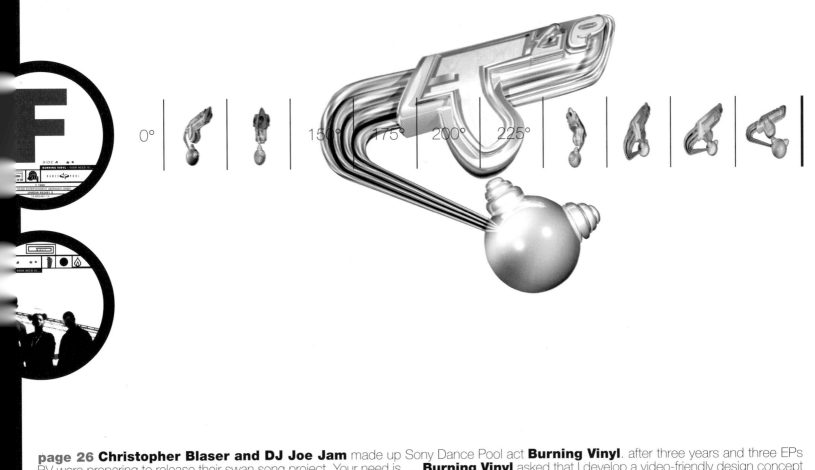

0° | 150° | 175° | 200° | 225°

page 26 Christopher Blaser and DJ Joe Jam made up Sony Dance Pool act **Burning Vinyl**. after three years and three EPs BV were preparing to release their swan song project, Your need is... . **Burning Vinyl** asked that I develop a video-friendly design concept and cover. just before the label Talk'in Loud came onto the scene cover designs for house consisted mostly of a logo stamped onto a white label. in Germany house music was just beginning a resurgence so I wanted to create something that would stand out in the coming crowd of releases. once released the track didn't do as well as expected so any plans for a video were scrapped. **page 27** this gun was used in the video I produced for **Tokyo Ghetto Pussy**. the original TGP logo was a hand rendered type treatment in the shape of a gun. before finishing video production I thought it would be interesting to bring the flat 2-dimensional logo to life. **page 28** I began using 3-D generated maps for designing labels for an **energy drink** that never made it to market. C'est la vie. **page 29** these three posters were commissioned for the German shoe company, **Goertz**, through the Hamburg advertising agency, Springer & Jacoby. **page 29 Zoom** was a rave held in Frankfurt. 3-D generated images on an event promotion. even though I worked with a computer operator in rendering this image I had to first learn the ins and outs of the program. the hours that I put in on this logo were worth it, as it was well received by the client. **page 29** one of the driving themes behind **Stephan Galloway's** planned magazine, Slave to the Empire, was sex. Galloway wanted something bold and in your face so I designed a heraldic symbol depicting sexual organs.

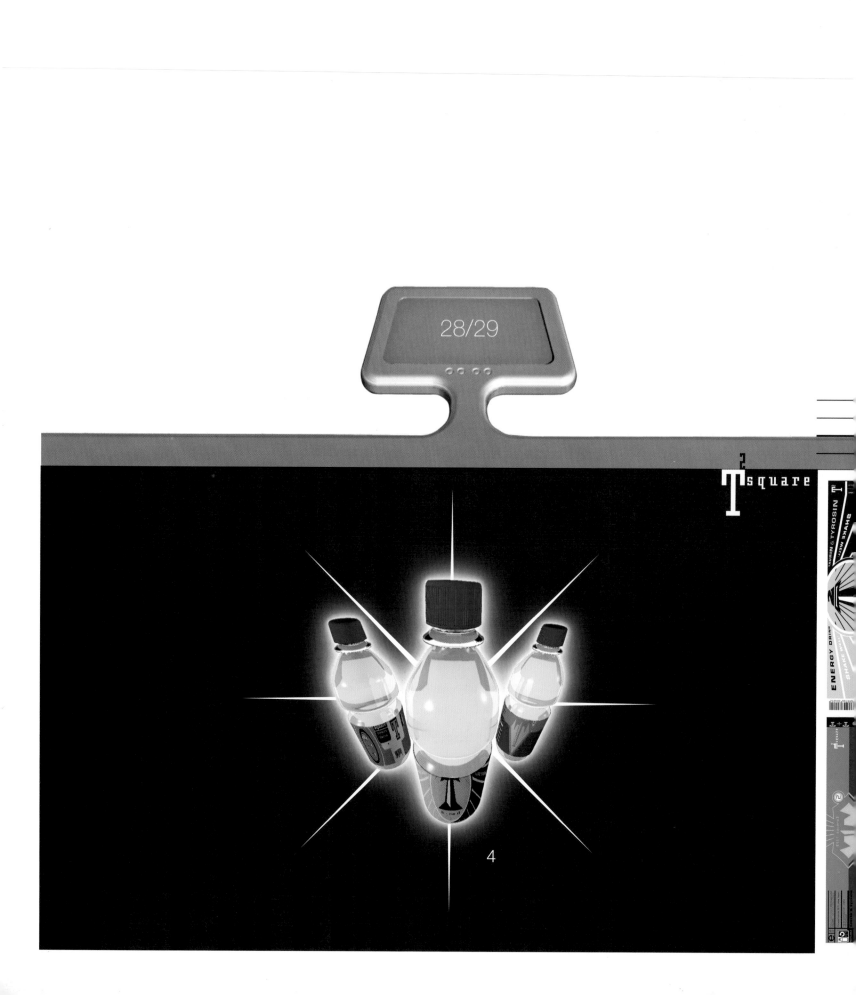

4

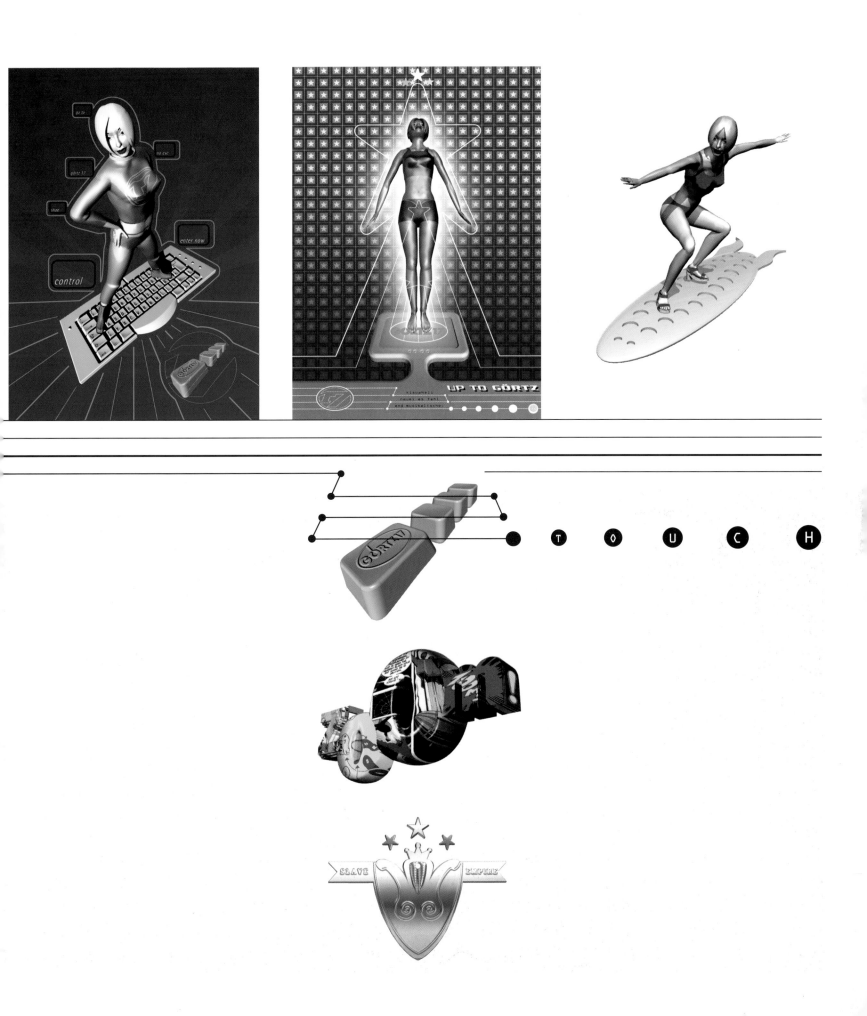

3

MISSION**LOGO**

ntroducing identity into a faceless world

hen I have to work out logos I almost always interject a level of humor. the fifty or so **logos** included here range from representing a music artist
the corporate identity to DSG, Germany's train company.

MISSION

Markus Löffel and Rolf Elmer were the producers behind **Jam & Spoon**. known for the remixes for Heaven 17, Qui[n]... Jones, Pet Shop Boys and Age of Love, J&S were about to release their debut, a double album. in the beginning working dire[ct]... with the group was made easier by the artists' open minds. over the course of two and half years and three singles the artis[t']... vision and mine began taking decidedly different paths. after completing the remix cover for the single Angel my involvement w[ith]... Jam & Spoon came to an end. all in all it's rare for a designer to work with good music and have creative freedom. in the ca[se]... of Jam & Spoon's **Tripomatic Fairytale 2001 and 2002**, as a designer I had the best of both worlds.

JAM & SPOON

apping the uncharted land of tripomatic fairytales

JAM & SPOON - TRIPOMATIC FAIRYTALES

"Alice in Wonderland" was my first response, since the music from the album was described as a non-stop psychedelic ride. designed a special CD package as well as taking advantage of extra colors. I was really allowed to cut loose on this project experimenti with colors and type treatments. being my first major cover design I went to great lengths to give each release, whether it was a sing or remix cover, a distinct style. another first was **Jam & Spoon**, a producer group, allowing themselves to be included in the cov art as well as the promotions. most of the cover projects that I'd previously completed involved an artist's logo and title. so having t chance to work visually with the artist was a real learning experience. after the album and first single release there was a break of almo a year before the second single, **Find Me (Odyssey to Anyoona)**, was released. picking up on the Indian them of Anyoona I settled on a Hindu style lettering for the logo. I took the basic graphic treatment from t album cover and structured it into a maze, as to say **"find me"**. I was told later that **Plavka**, Jam & Spoon's primary singer, was be included on the cover. I thought changing the crystal ball layout would never work so I made Plavka into a dancing Shiva. **Ang** the third single was released once again a year after the previous one. taking a base image of J&S created for the album I transform into an angel. out of all of the work this single was the simplest design and the easiest to do. the finished work was a dramatic chan for cover designs coming out of Germany and set a new direction for my style of design.

discographie

tripomatic fairytàles 2001
tripomatic fairytales 2002
right in the night
flamenc-o-matic fairytales (remixes)
the remixes
find me (odysee to anchoona)
angel

best medicine the doctor gave to me, first I felt sick, now I feel **free**

2001

the **joint**-venture

adventure

of jam & spoon

01

02

03

08

09

10

11

16

17

18

19

24

25

26

27

04

05

06

07

12

13

14

15

20

21

22

23

28

29

30

31

40

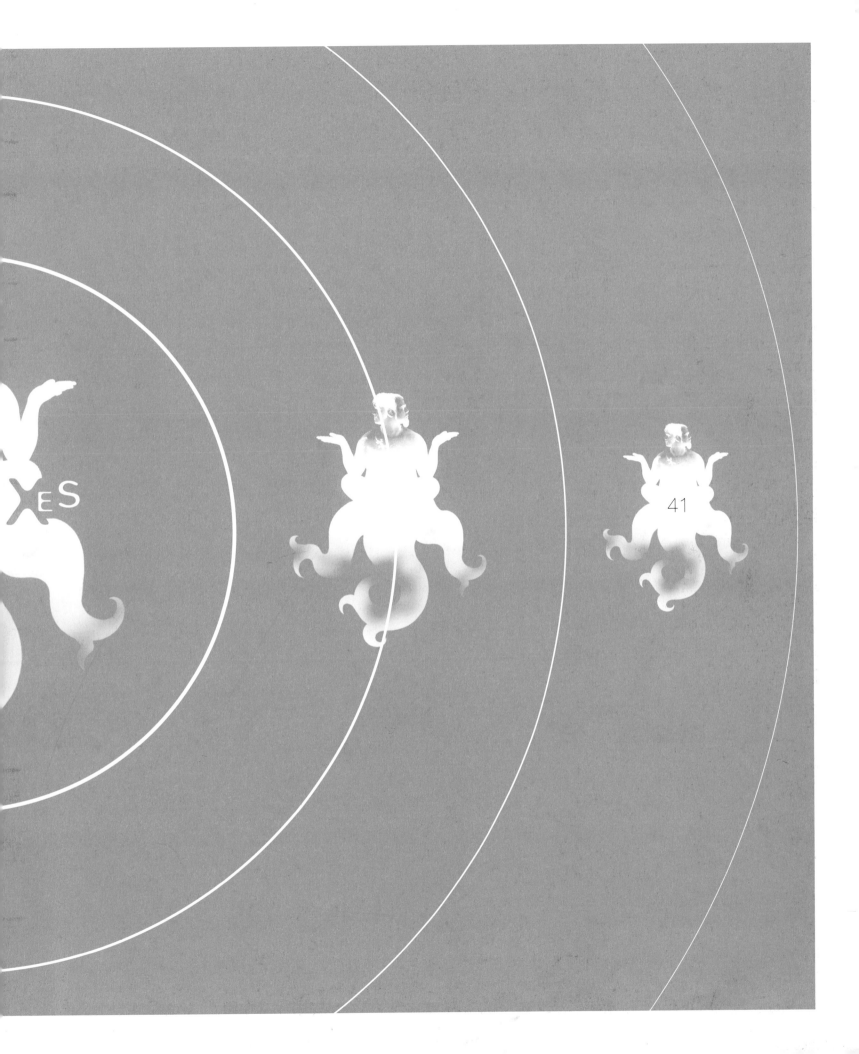

41

42

1

(2001)

spoonilum and jamdidei

made us twins with just one eye

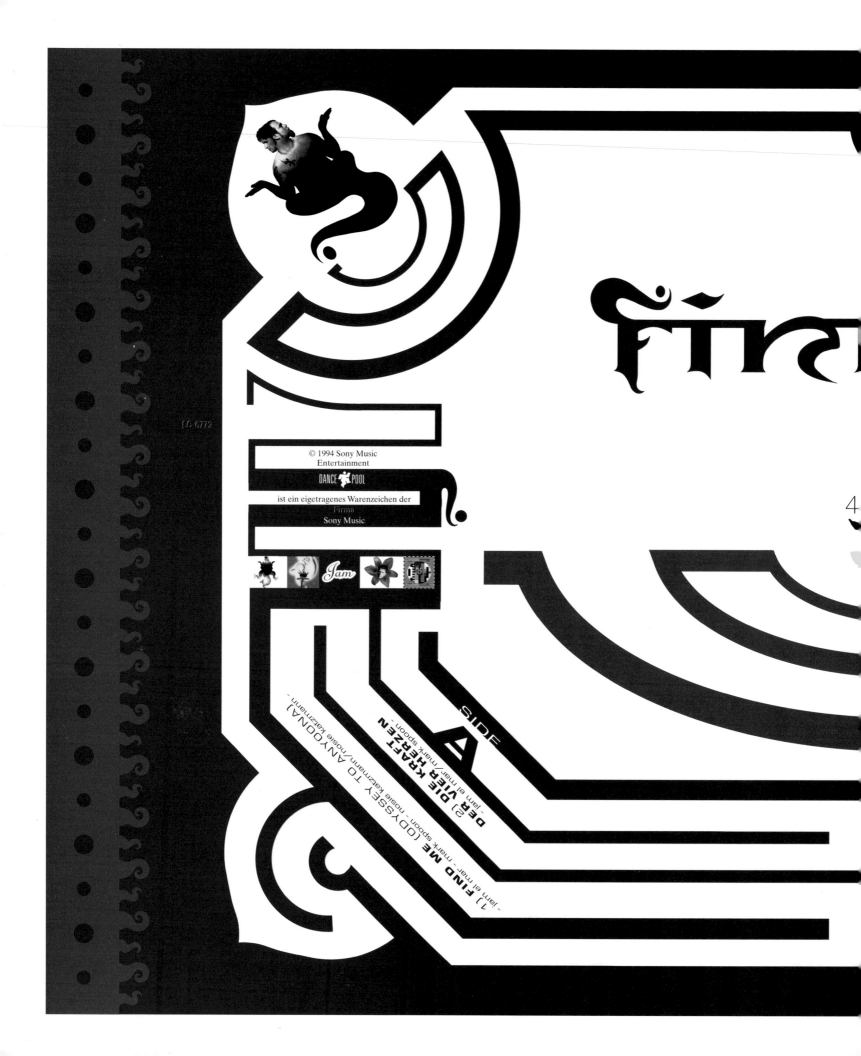

firm

LG 6772

4

SIDE

A

1) **FIND ME** (ODYSSEY TO ANYDONA)
- jam el mar - mark spoon -

2) **DER VIER HERZEN**
- jam el mar - nosie katzmann -

3) **DIE KRAFT**
- jam el mar / mark spoon -

4) **DIE KRAFT / nosie katzmann** -

DANCE POOL

jam!

SIDE B

1) THE TRIBE
- jam el mar - christoph blaser -

2) ODYSSEY TO ANYOONA
- jam el mar - mark spoon - noise katzmann -

- jam el mar - mark spoon -

don't stop

in addition to the larger, more complex projects, there have been many smaller jobs that kept in my hog. included here are record covers that pre-date my Jam & Spoon material by about three years, some of pre-KM7 and Trust work as well as several advertising projects.

MISSIONINTHEMIX

ving aid to all in need

HOT

from the very

moment

an

idea

is born

a

guardian angel

stands by it's side to

guide and protect it

on a long and

exciting journey

17. - 20. AUGUST 1995 POPKOMM HALLE 14.1
STAND B3

Sony Music Publishing
Germany

get me going

(H(E(A(R(T A T T)A)C)K)

IS IS MY LIFE (137 BASS KICK MIX) 5:55   THIS IS MY LIFE (PUMPIN' 142 BPM)

IS IS MY LIFE (MEGAHERTZ MIX) 3:45   THIS IS MY LIFE (SPACE OUT MIX)

DAN 660361 6

DANCE POOL

LC 6772

4 Sony Music Entertainment (Germany) GmbH/
DANCE POOL

ein eingetragenes Warenzeichen der Firma
usic Entertainment Inc./Distribution Sony Music
12-660381-20

5 099766 339764

music & lyrics by **CHRIS CRAFT**

rap lyrics by **ERIC B.**

produced by **CHRIS CRAFT FOR
MEDIAPOOL**

sirius & chris craft managed by
MEDIAAGENCY WAGNER & PARTNER

publisher: **COPYRIGHT CONTROL**

7

8

9

10

15

16

17

21

22

23

27

28

29

30

page 50 I created the logo for **God's Favorite Dog** as an integral part of the cover. **page 51 Boom** was my first work done for Sony and to this day one of my favorite pieces. **page 52** in 1994 **Sony Music Publishing** came to me for an image ad that included their house/office, which everyone was proud of, in Frankfurt. the ad went well and I was then asked to develop a new identity to be used for Sony Music Publishing World Wide. what I presented was a logo depicting SMP as a **guardian angel**. They kept the guardian angel tag line and passed on the logo. **page 53** the TV series, **Real Life**, released a compilation of current music used on the show and my cover used obvious television elements.

11

12

13

14

18

19

20

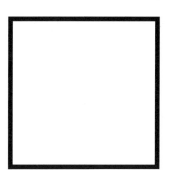

24

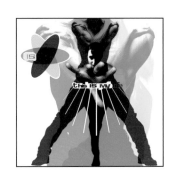

25

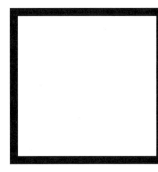

26

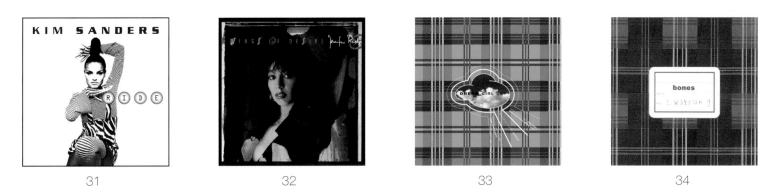

31

32

33

34

page 54 for this **Heart Attack** cover I altered a set of ears into the shape of the heart. this Heart Attack cover was done for Intercord Records. **page 55** on the **Sirus** cover I took elements from a digital code used by scientists in an attempt to contact life in outer space. **page 56+57** some of the many single covers from the last five years. **page 58** I developed a logo and cover for artist **Biz**, which I later used for a series of ads. **page 59 Nike** wanted a watch designed to give-a-way at one of their international marketing meetings in Orlando. I never got a watch. **page 60 Lektion 1** cover produced for Electrola. **page 61** Design elements for a new **Ford car, Ka**.

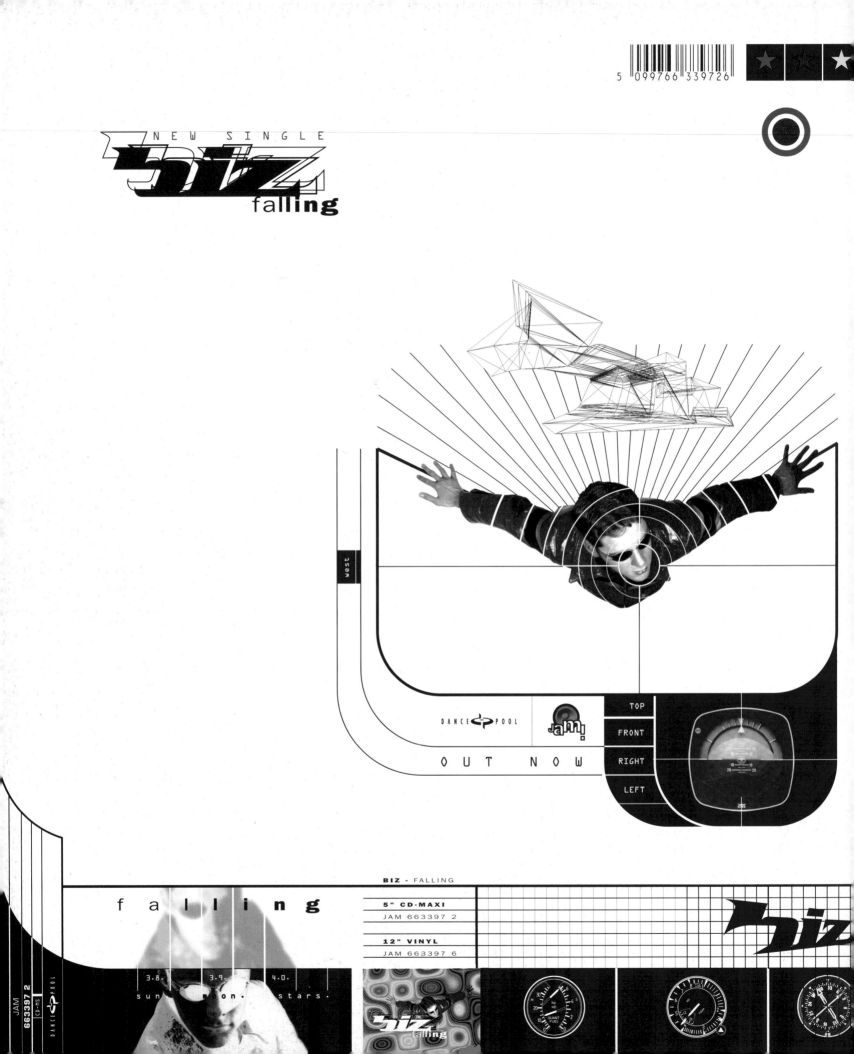

TIME TRAVEL

SWOOSH

LONDON   PARIS   MILANO   NEW YORK   TOKYO

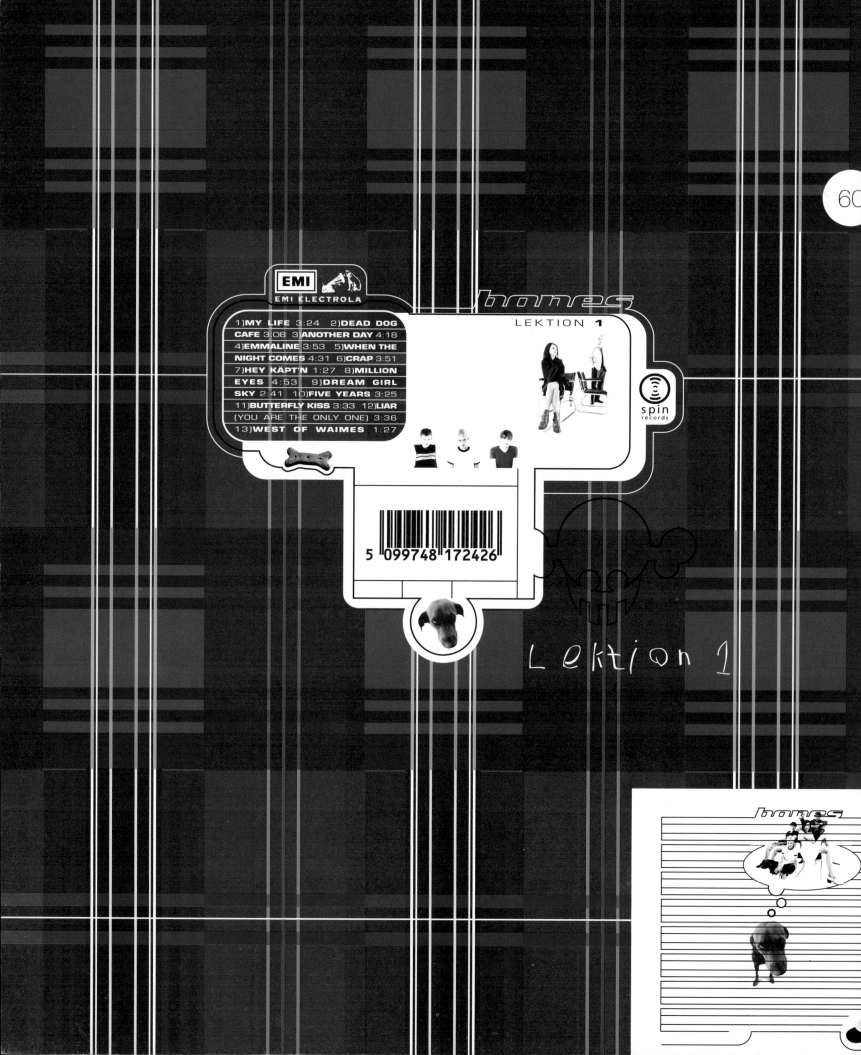

EMI
EMI ELECTROLA

bones

LEKTION **1**

1)**MY LIFE** 3:24 2)**DEAD DOG**
CAFE 3:08 3)**ANOTHER DAY** 4:18
4)**EMMALINE** 3:53 5)**WHEN THE**
NIGHT COMES 4:31 6)**CRAP** 3:51
7)**HEY KÄPT'N** 1:27 8)**MILLION**
EYES 4:53 9)**DREAM GIRL**
SKY 2:41 10)**FIVE YEARS** 3:25
11)**BUTTERFLY KISS** 3:33 12)**LIAR**
(YOU ARE THE ONLY ONE) 3:36
13)**WEST OF WAIMES** 1:27

spin
records

5 099748 172426

Lektion 1

bones

Ka vrooooom

S P E E D

U P

vroooom

40

Buffalo

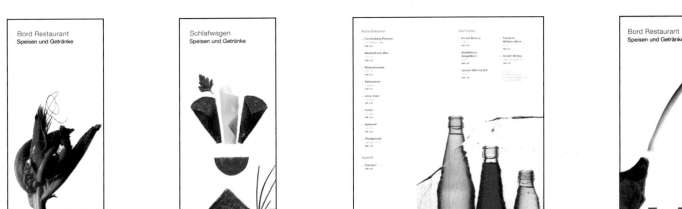

Bord Restaurant
Speisen und Getränke

Schlafwagen
Speisen und Getränke

Kalte Getränke

Bord Restaurant
Speisen und Getränke

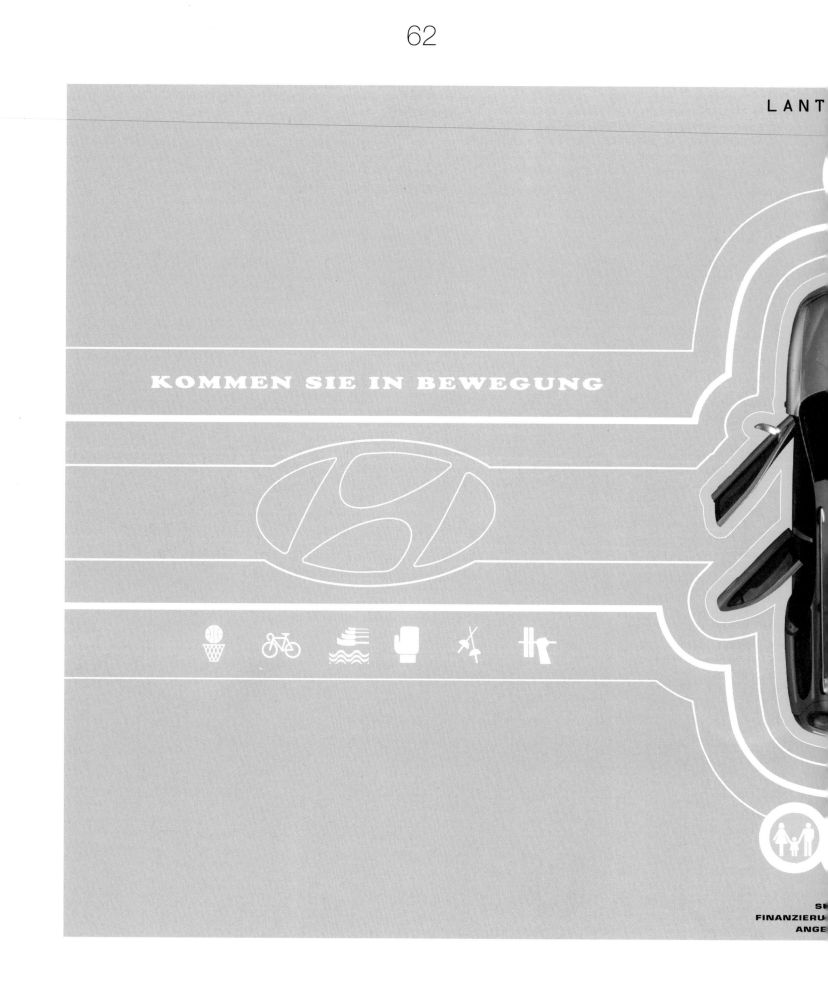

LANT

KOMMEN SIE IN BEWEGUNG

SI
FINANZIERU
ANGE

MBI

DER NEUE **HYUNDI LANTRA
KOMBI** IST DA.
FREIZEITAKTIV
SCHON AB **25.990,-DM*** M
UMFANGREICHER
SERIENAUSSTATTUNG.

HYUNDAI
LIFE LIVE

0,9% EFFEKTIVER
ESZINS. (36
ATE LAUFZEIT, 20%
HLUNG)

page 61 I art directed these illustrations for a series of ads for a German shoe company, **Buffalo Boots**.   **page 61** the German-owned tr
system, DSG, commissioned me to redesign their food service identity. DSG and Buffalo Boots were both projects I completed while serving ti
at Trust.   **page 62+63** a local ad agency called upon me to develop graphics for their client **Hyundai**. they wanted something that pushed
limits of Hyundai's current campaign. in the end the client took the new approach for a newer line of cars, but two weeks later dropped the agen
page 64 this logo and package were designed for a California Cosmetic company and also won **Best Package Design** in Mexi
page 65 the **World Frisbee Championship** was being held in Tokyo and this design represented the German National team.

MISSION

guiding two legends **to the dancefloors of europe**
Motor Music organized this special **Yello** tribute project. fifteen of Europe's most influential producers and remixers were as to remix their favorite Yello track. being a long-time fan of Yello, I agreed to the project before actually thinking how much work it wo

HANDS ON YELLO

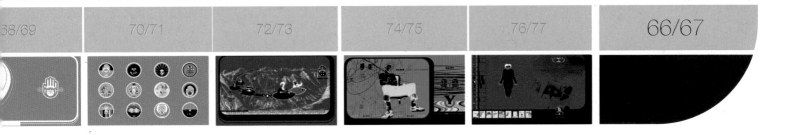

each of the fifteen tracks I created special artwork which
as used on the CD booklet as well as the individual releases.
sed Silver as an extra color and the logo was embossed.

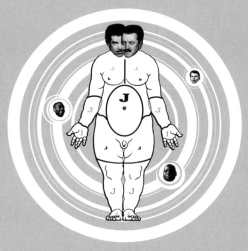

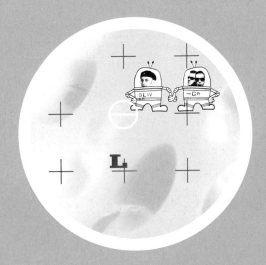

HandsonYello

LER TURBO

FAFLER

BLATTEN

RIED

ELL

JEN

5:40   3:06   5:17   5:50

IEL OUVERT

4:45   5:38

74/75

BORiS   DiETeR

OLIVER LIEB

you gotta say **yes** to another excess

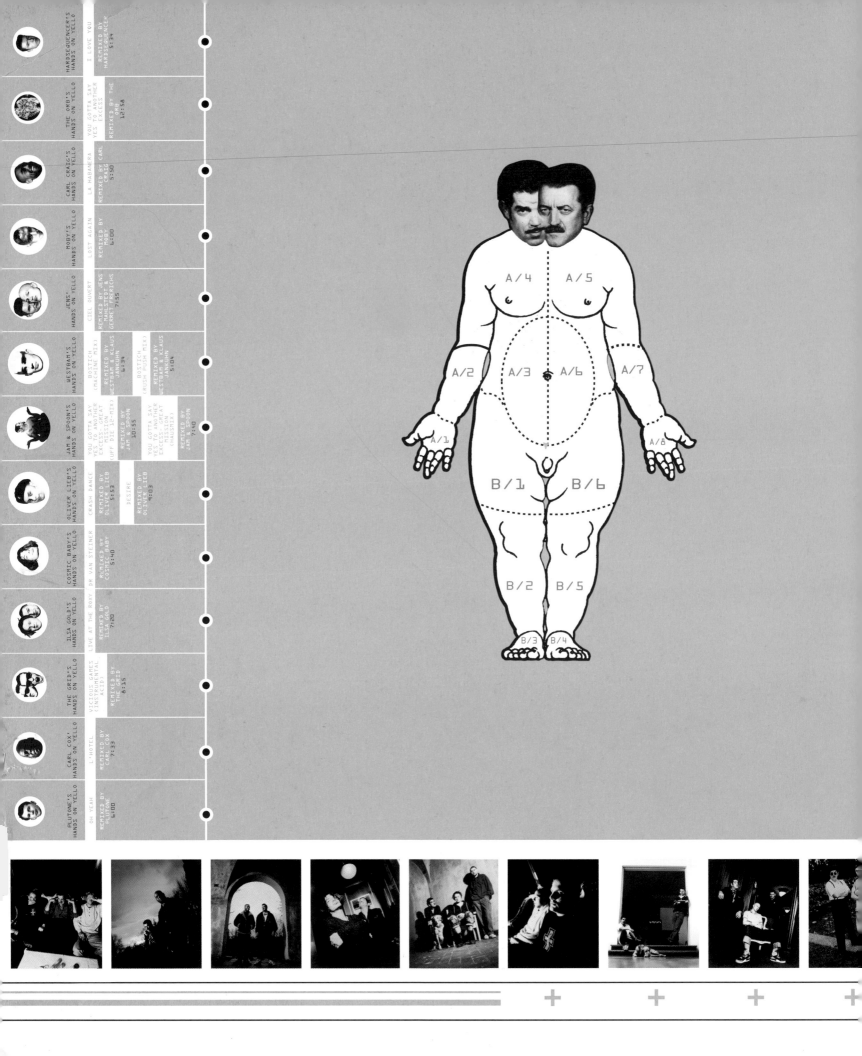

HARDSEQUENCER'S
HANDS ON YELLO
I LOVE YOU
REMIXED BY
HARDSEQUENCER
5:34

THE ORB'S
HANDS ON YELLO
YOU GOTTA SAY
YES TO ANOTHER
EXCESS
REMIXED BY THE
ORB
12:56

CARL CRAIG'S
HANDS ON YELLO
LA HABANERA
REMIXED BY CARL
CRAIG
5:50

MOBY'S
HANDS ON YELLO
LOST AGAIN
REMIXED BY
MOBY
6:00

JENS'
HANDS ON YELLO
CIEL OUVERT
REMIXED BY JENS
MAHLSTEDT &
GERRET FRERICHS
7:55

WESTBAM'S
HANDS ON YELLO
BOSTICH
(MACHINE MIX)
REMIXED BY
WESTBAM & KLAUS
JANKUHN
6:34

BOSTICH
(RUSH PUSH MIX)
REMIXED BY
WESTBAM & KLAUS
JANKUHN
5:04

JAM & SPOON'S
HANDS ON YELLO
YOU GOTTA SAY
YES TO ANOTHER
EXCESS- GREAT
MISSION
(UFF DIE 12-MIX)
REMIXED BY
JAM & SPOON
10:55

YOU GOTTA SAY
YES TO ANOTHER
EXCESS- GREAT
MISSION
(HAUSMIX)
REMIXED BY
JAM & SPOON
7:40

OLIVER LIEB'S
HANDS ON YELLO
CRASH DANCE
REMIXED BY
OLIVER LIEB
5:53

DESIRE
REMIXED BY
OLIVER LIEB
9:03

COSMIC BABY'S
HANDS ON YELLO
DR VAN STEINER
REMIXED BY
COSMIC BABY
5:40

ILSA GOLD'S
HANDS ON YELLO
LIVE AT THE ROXY
REMIXED BY
ILSA GOLD
7:20

THE GRID'S
HANDS ON YELLO
VICIOUS GAMES
(INSTRUMENTAL
ACID)
REMIXED BY
THE GRID
8:15

CARL COX'
HANDS ON YELLO
L'HOTEL
REMIXED BY
CARL COX
7:33

PLUTONE'S
HANDS ON YELLO
OH YEAH
REMIXED BY
PLUTONE
6:00

A/4   A/5

A/2   A/3   A/6   A/7

A/1   A/8

B/1   B/6

B/2   B/5

B/3   B/4

7

PAX

P
—
A
—
X

MISSIONPAX24

bringing peace to the world with a simple meal

the **dishware company WMF** asked me to design a dinnerware collection to be brought out sometime around Christmas. I took the Latin word for peace, pax and the numerical date 24, when most Europeans celebrate Christmas, to for **pax24**. for presentation purposes I had 3-D renderings made of the actual plates. this turned out to be invaluable in getting a detailed view of my designs without having to produce sample plates.

FILE #SEVEN

PUSS

WILD

delivering unto the charts **a new power ggr**

when Sony approached me to design the album and single for their new signing, **Tokyo Ghetto Pussy**, they orig
wanted something simple, black and silver with an embossing. at the time Akira and other Japanese Animi were g
exposure through the German club scene, so I used some of those elements when creating little Miss TGP. I intentio
made my character rude, since her representing a techno band being cute just wouldn't work. everyone at Sony
happy with it and after digging in my heels, so were the producers. Sony pushed the first single with several remixes
even more DJ promos, each requiring a different cover.

MISSIONTOKYO

8

86/87

FILE #EIGHT

GHETTO PUSSY

tokyo ghetto

STEREO

to: another
Galaxy

90/91

ジャム＆スプーン

TOKYO GHETTO PUSSY

（PUMP IT）

EVERYBODY ON THE FLOOR

94/95

REMIXES

A		F		L		Q		V	
B		G		M		R		W	
C		H		N		S		X	
D		I		O		T		Y	
E		K		P		U		Z	

スプーン
ジャム

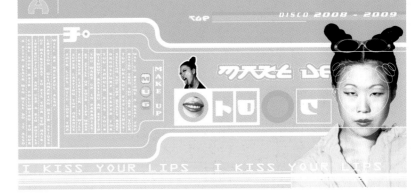

I KISS YOUR LIPS   I KISS YOUR LIPS

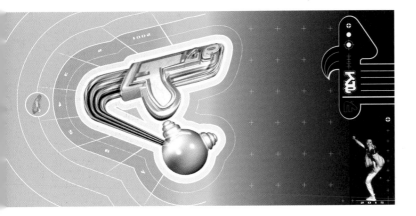

DISCO

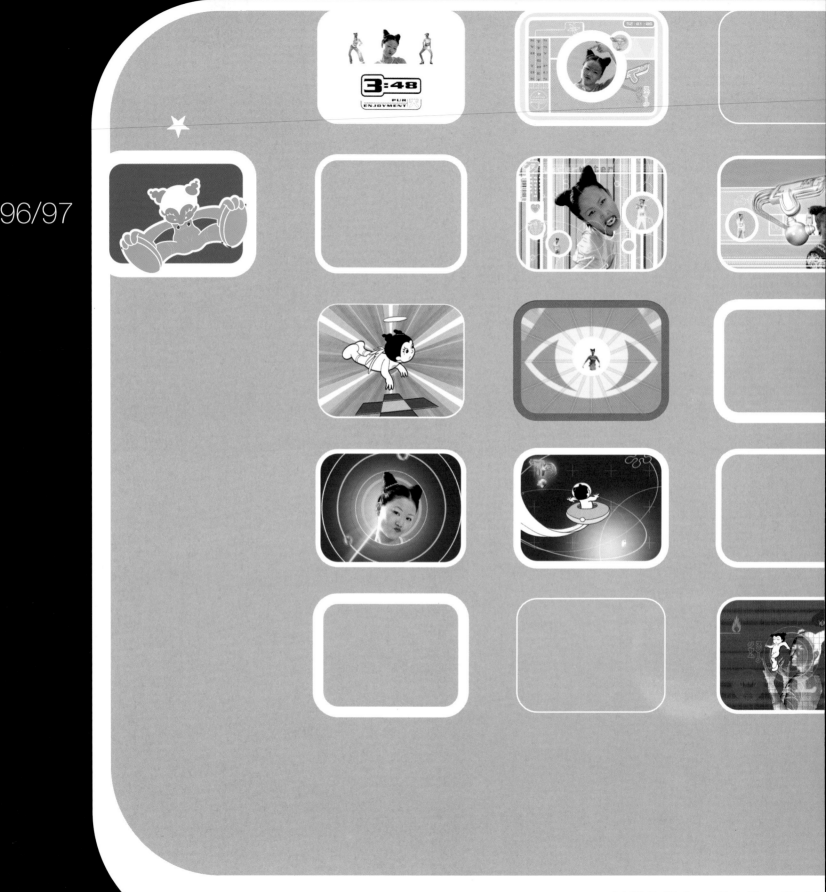

The first single and video didn't come out as well as Sony would have liked, so I was asked to produce the next video, as I was already working on the cover. Being unimpressed with most of the computer-generated video on the air at the time, I wanted to do something more interesting and intelligent. I was able to apply stop action animation to the figure and worked out several 3-D images and backgrounds. Sony thought that the album and the video needed a person to front the group in order to make it more appealing to fans. **All in all the video combined stop action animation, live footage and typography.** I was very pleased with this work as it was the first music project where I was able to art direct the cover, promotions and video. I only wish the music had been of the same quality...or at least near it.

KISS YOUR LIPS

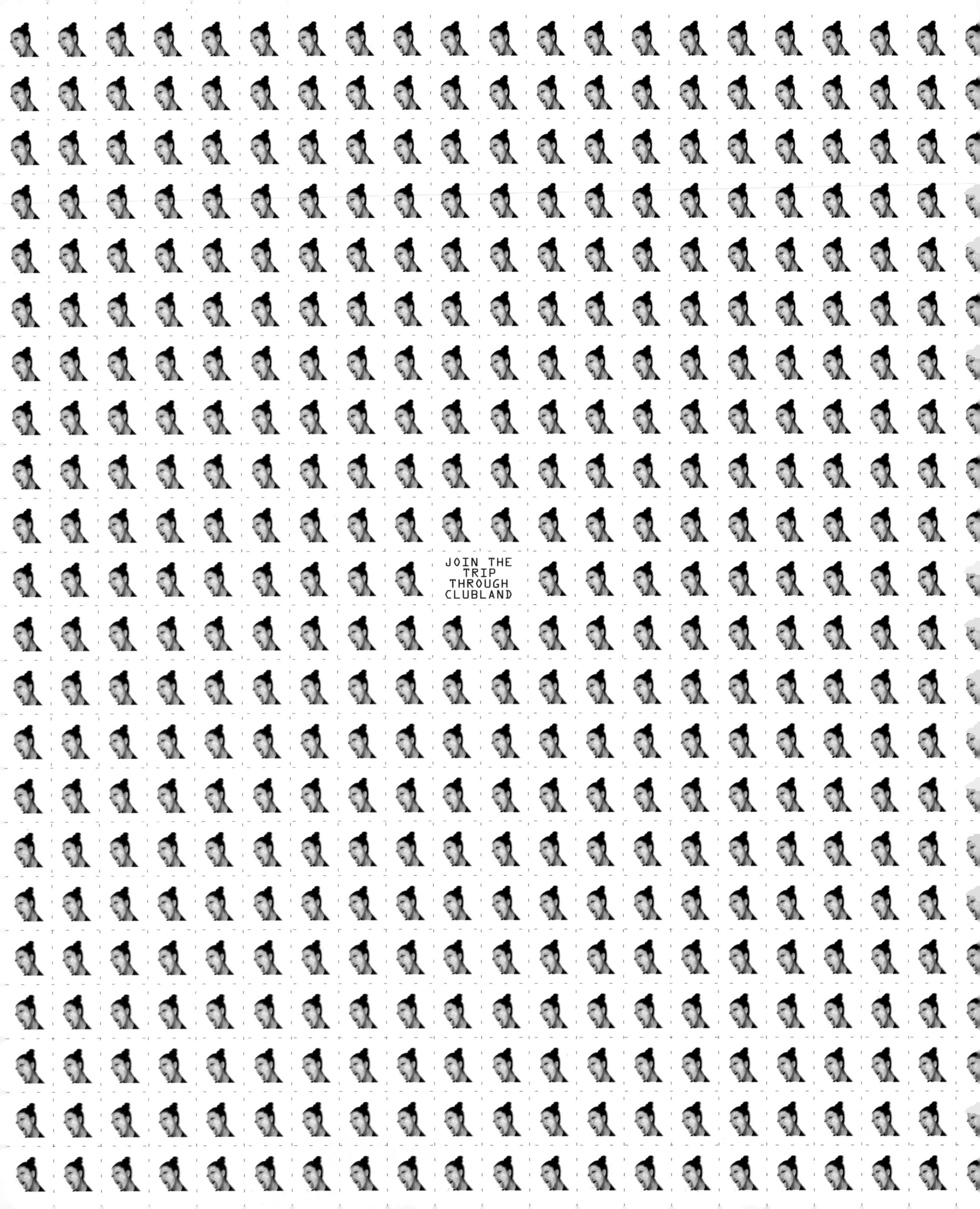

JOIN THE
TRIP
THROUGH
CLUBLAND

LICK
IT

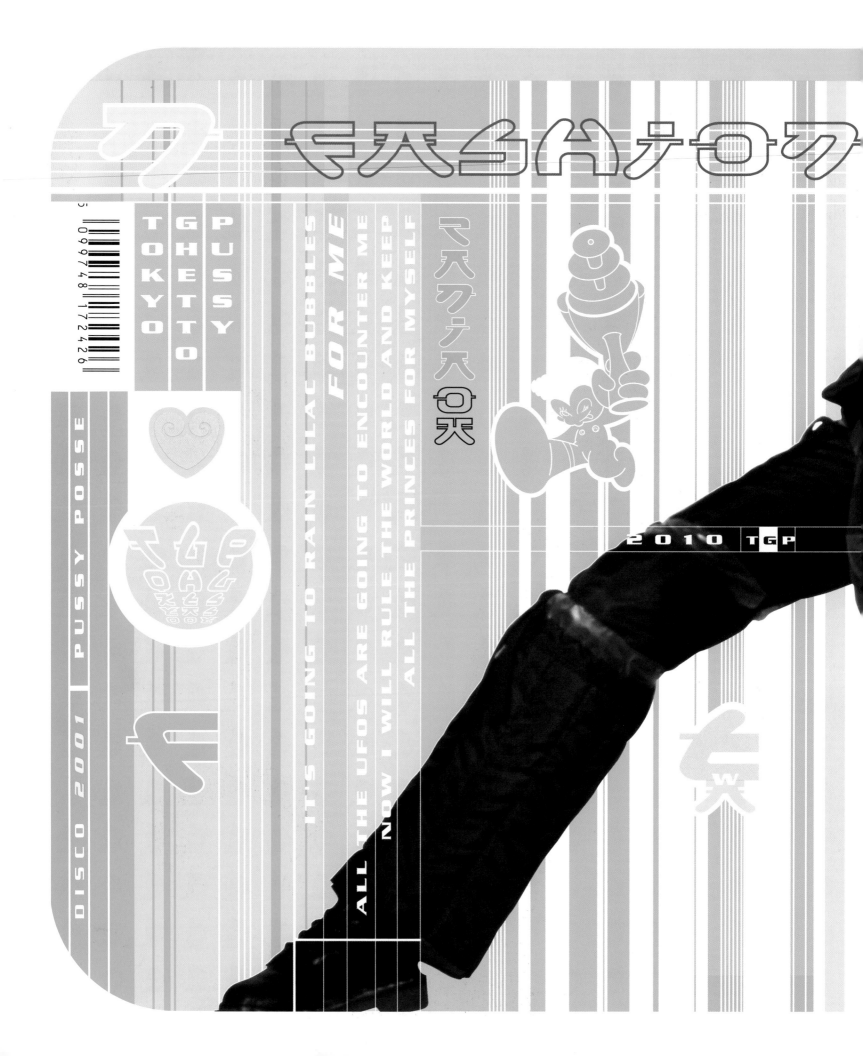

FASHION *2010 -2011*

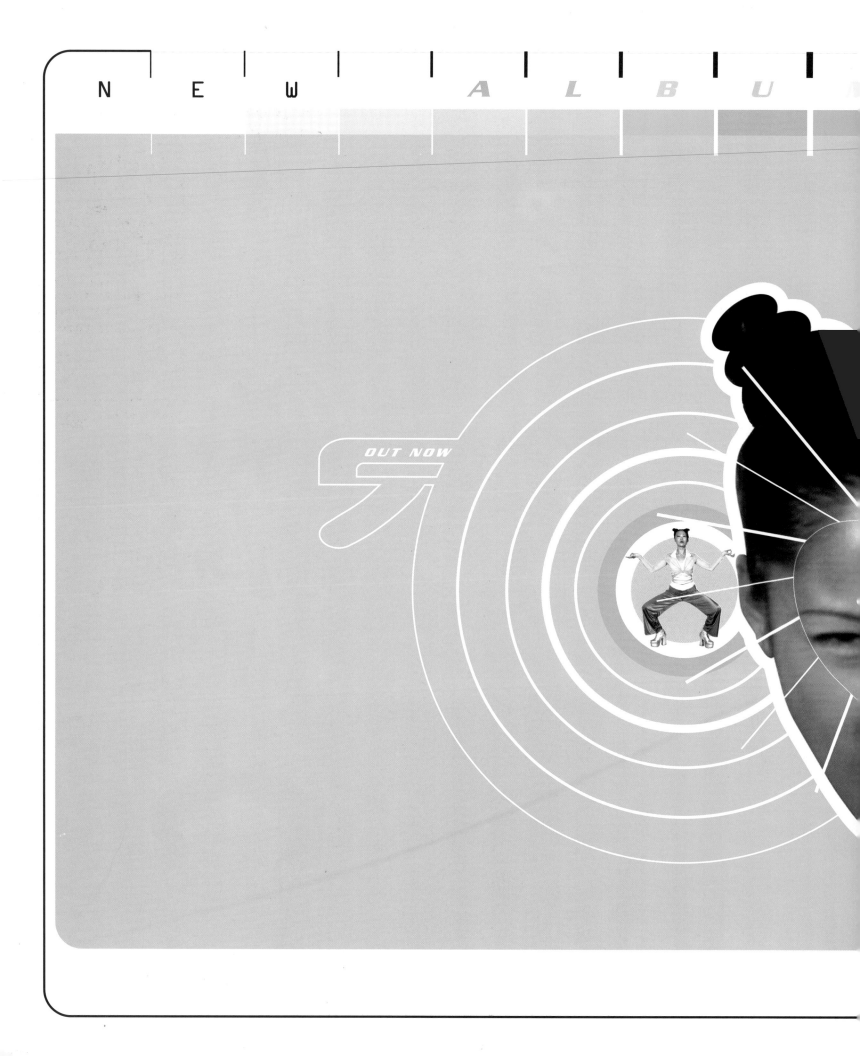

OUT NOW

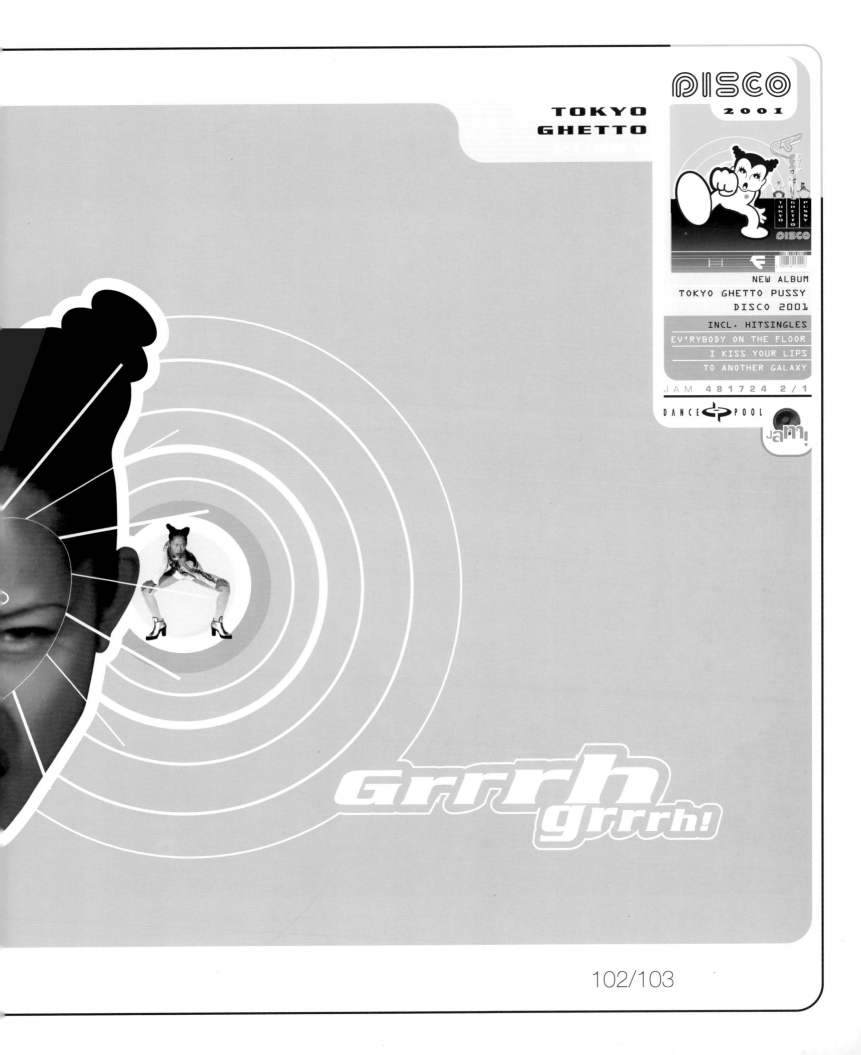

MISSION

in the techno playground of Frankfurt, Germany, a new house opened up, **Club XS**. DJ/producer Markus Löffel and his partner in c
Alex Azary took their old alias, Sound Factory, and buried it. their new nightspot was a cavern which brought with it the sounds of
underground. while techno ruled the land, XS let loose new st

CLUB XS

9

ushing the boundaries and looking good too

XS – FUTURE CLUBBING

with guest DJs, live bands and special parties the short existence of **XS infused Frankfurt's night with new life**. what I attempted do was create a visual identity that reflected the diversity and energy behind XS. the club was opened five days a week and needed invitati for at least 10 events each month. the club owners wanted to create attention for the club, so the invites I designed involved everything fr die-cuts, extra colors, folds and even condoms. though the money from my two years as sole designer of XS wasn't much, I was really lu to be able to have that kind of exposure at a time in which I needed new projects.

XS

alex**azary** / markus**löffel**

dive into the **ultra**world

NO
DICKS
ALLOWED
!!!

night of the holy sluts - party '92

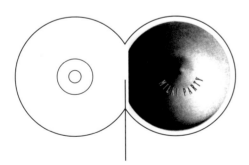

milk party '92

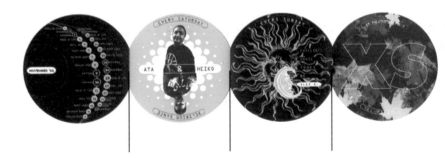

program nov.92

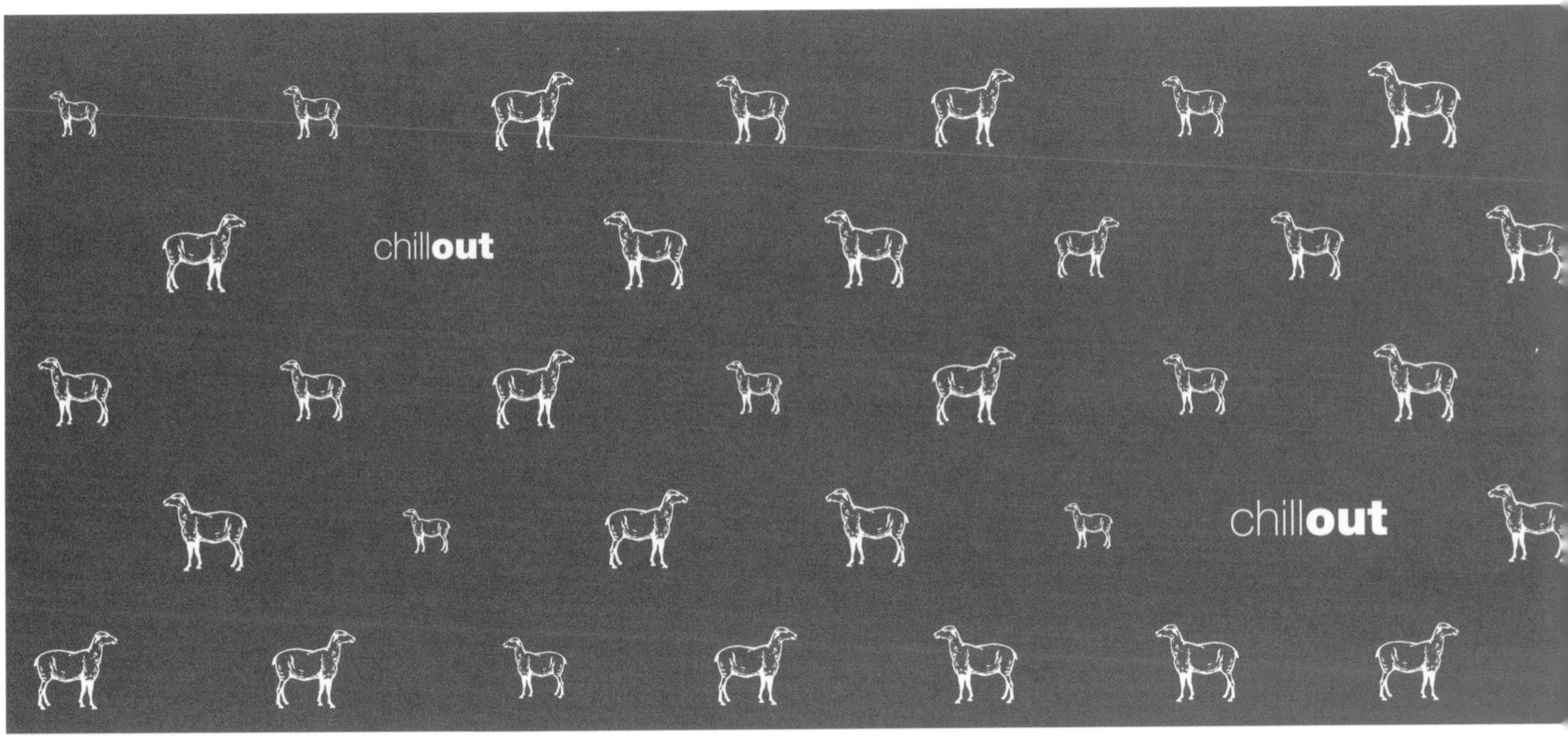

chillout

chillout

12

13

14

of Alex Patterson's Orb which became the template for most of today's trance and amibent movement. in addition to their regular w
line-up the XS through birthday parties and events XS brought together a who's who of Frankfurt's nightlife. in its five-year existen
enjoyed the status of being a major player in shaping club culture in Frankfurt, Germany, and as far away as London. though the

welcome

chill**out**

8 9 10 11

became the hangout for record label types. The best part of this entire job is that every night had a different feel and that called variety of designs. Another popular night was Sunday, ChillOut. It was XS that actually took the after-hours get-together out of the e and into club. For the first month they brought in, on Sundays only, some straw and a live sheep. This was all in reaction to the

chill**out**

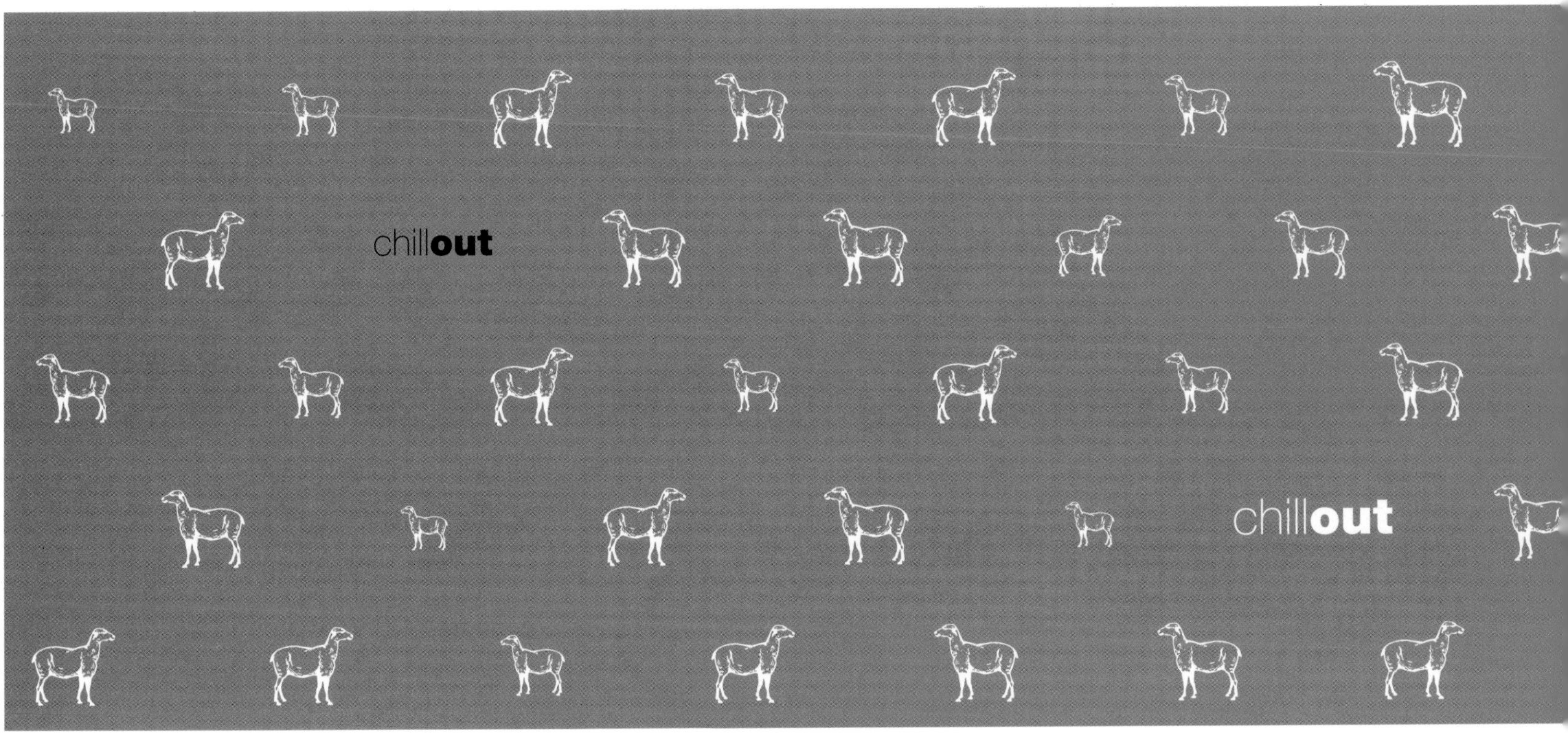

chillout

chillout

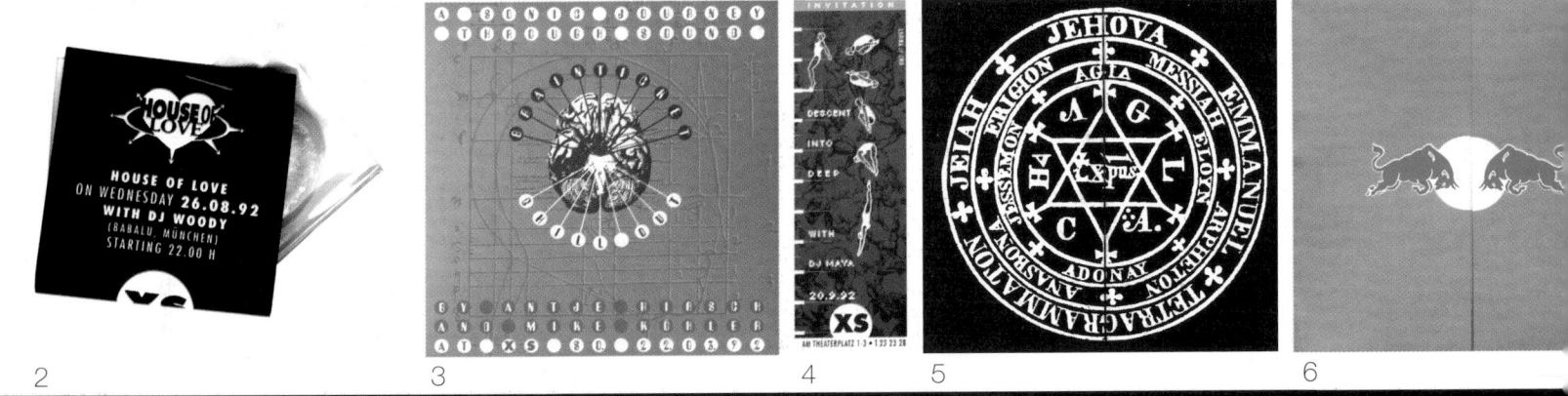

2 3 4 5 6

What made XS a legend in Frankfurt, and most of Germany, was its commitment to create something new and have it continue to e[v]
From the very beginning the club introduced five nights, each with its own unique theme. Wednesday became a House of Love
featured garage house and became one of the club's most successful night. At the time Wednesdays normally saw little traffic, b[u]

chill**out**

1

lub XS was an idea before its time, as a result it only lasted for two years.
its short life XS managed to re-invent the Frankfurt nightlife by offering five
ights of house, breakbeats, techno, chillout and live acts.
eing a new club, it was important for the owners, Alex Azary and Markus Löffel
at any promotions representing XS were extravagant.

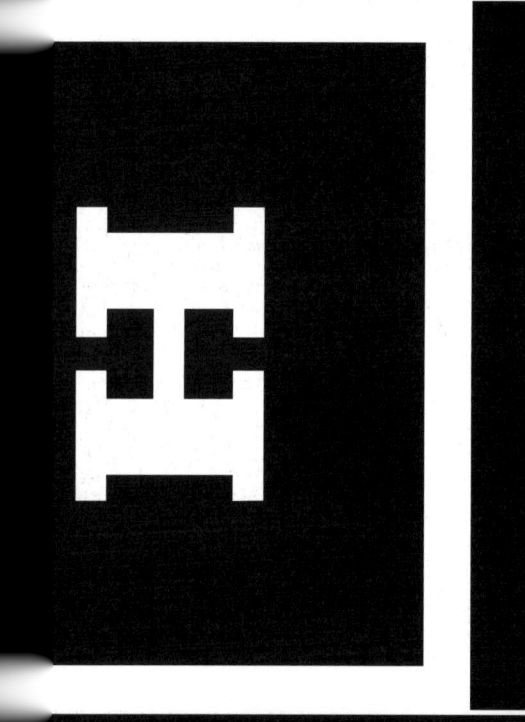

every saturday at **konstabler**

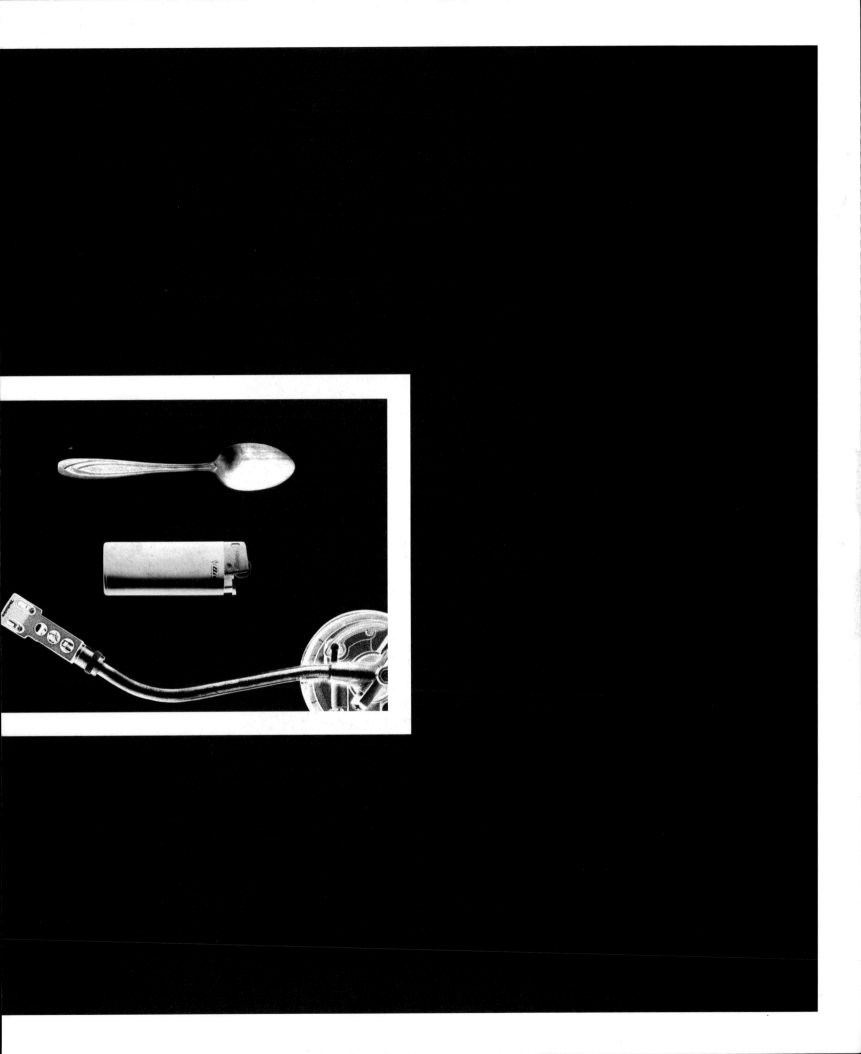

ore parties than you can throw a rave at.

on

DISCO

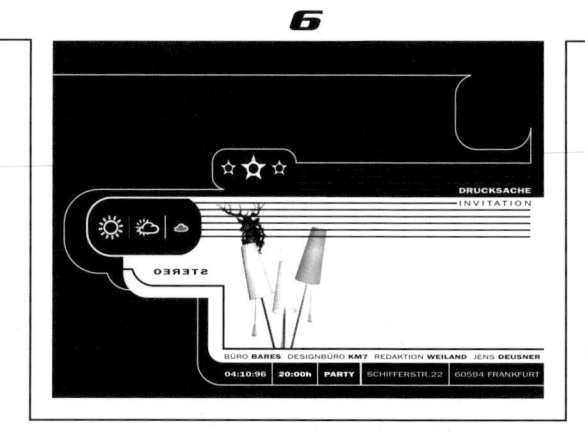

danish rave wave
1

party

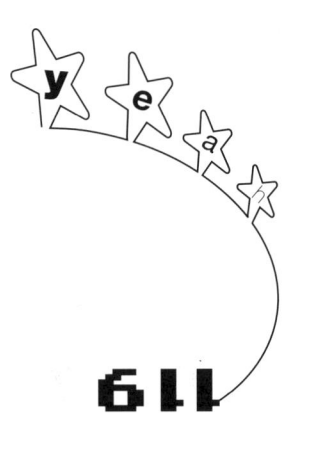

zoom rave   **palais osthafen**   cosmic trigger

The Zoom Rave was the first time I'd worked with 3-D graphics. After getting a crash course in using the system, waiting days for image rendering and receiving a very large bill, it was probably the last time. The Palais Osthafen was a summer event that was held from 1991-1993 and comprises some of my first invitation work.

Cosmic Trigger was the label given to an AIDS benefit project. The result was several parties and CD compilations

HOLY
CHRISTMAS
RAVE'93

□PRINZ
DIE ILLUSTRIERTE DER STADT
PRÄSENTIERT
3 jahre **hr3 clubnight**
karten im vorverkauf
franziusstr. 20 • frankfurt • 20.00 h
15.5.93

dj's: torsten fenslau
chilly t.
lady d.
heinz felber
sven vath

hr3

94

With the number of parties being planned on the increase, creating visuals that are eye-catching as well as memorable is essential. This problem is solved by keeping the main focus simple and direct.
With the Sylvester Weekend invite (roughly translated into New Year) a three-day rave at Frankfurt's infamous club at the airport, Dorian Gray, the flame idea reflects fireworks and festivities that normally accompany New Year's Eve.
A similar solution was used for the Holy Christmas rave and the cookie cutter.
HR3, a German radio station, celebrated their 3rd year annivesary with, what else, a party. Don't bother looking for any logic in this design, I didn't and the party was a success anyway.

journal FRANKFURT

sylvester rave **holy christmas rave** hr3 clubnight

sylvester *Weekend*

friday
31.12.93
-
sunday
02.01.94

at dorian gray
eintritt 28 DM

new years eve &
new years day in 3 clubs.

including indoor fireworks
& decoration

freier eintritt bei menue
bestellung

reservierung 069 - 690 221 21

31.12.93 -

new years eve & new years day in 3 clu

including indoor fireworks & decoration *at dorian g*

DJ **DAG**	DJ **TOM**	DJ **MARK SPOON**	DR **MOTTE**	DJ **SPEZIAL**	DJ **SAMMY**
DJ **MARKY B.**	**SHOOT**	DJ **TEAM**	DJ **T**	DJ **PUSSYLOVER**	DJ **HEIKO M/**
DJ **SILVIE**	DJ **NICO**	DJ **PIT**	DJ **ROMAN**	DJ **LUTZ**	DJ **JOE JAM**	*LIVE:* **RESISTAN**

n väth
Oj "T"
27 juli 92

alle after hours eintritt frei | wetterhotline 06181-255250

TK 35DM | VVK 28DM + VVK GEBÜHR

ANAU | Vorverkauf an allen bekannten VVK-
Stellen & Highnoon Records Hanau

sonntagsmesse

DUNLOP
VING TO THE FUTURE

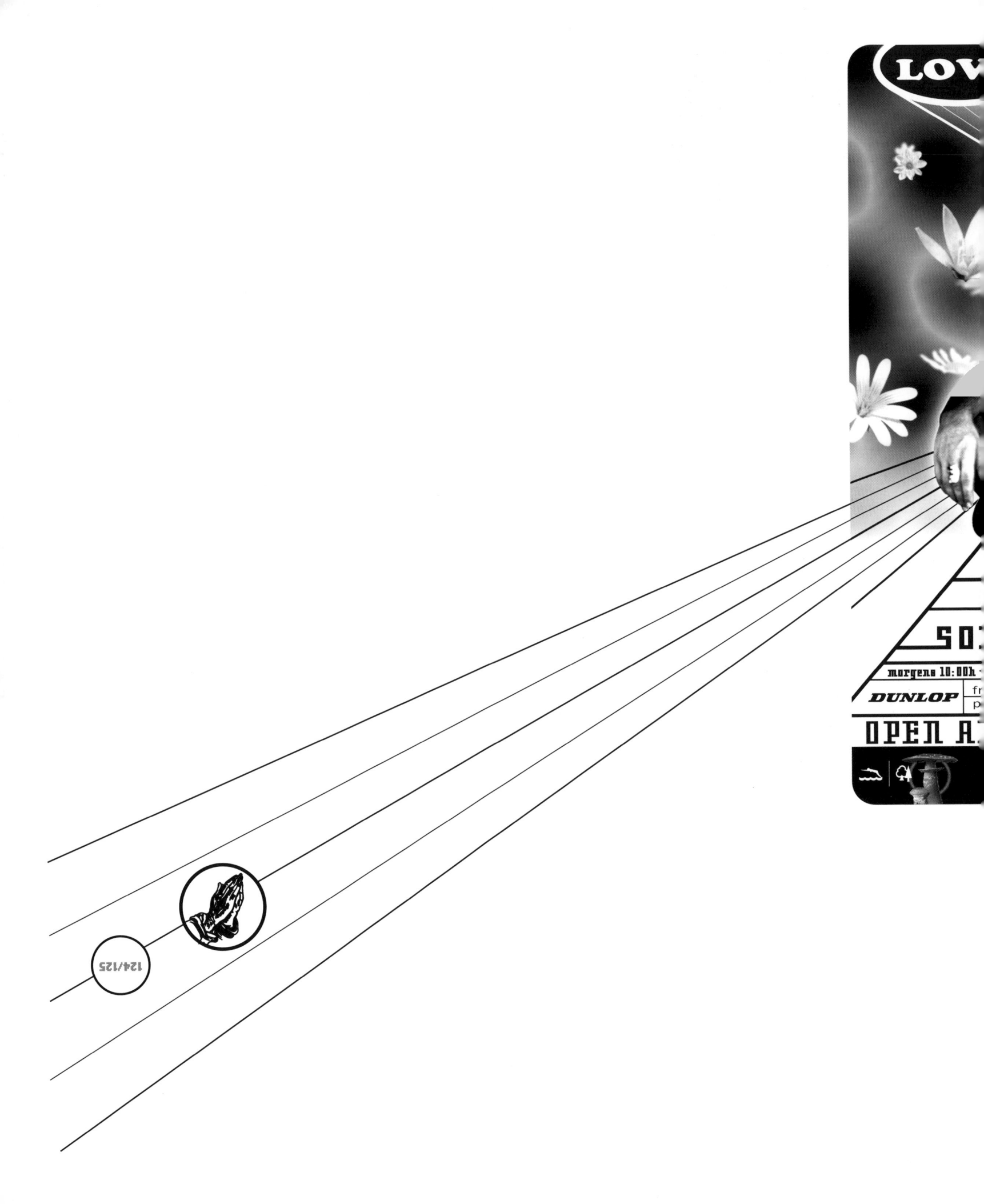

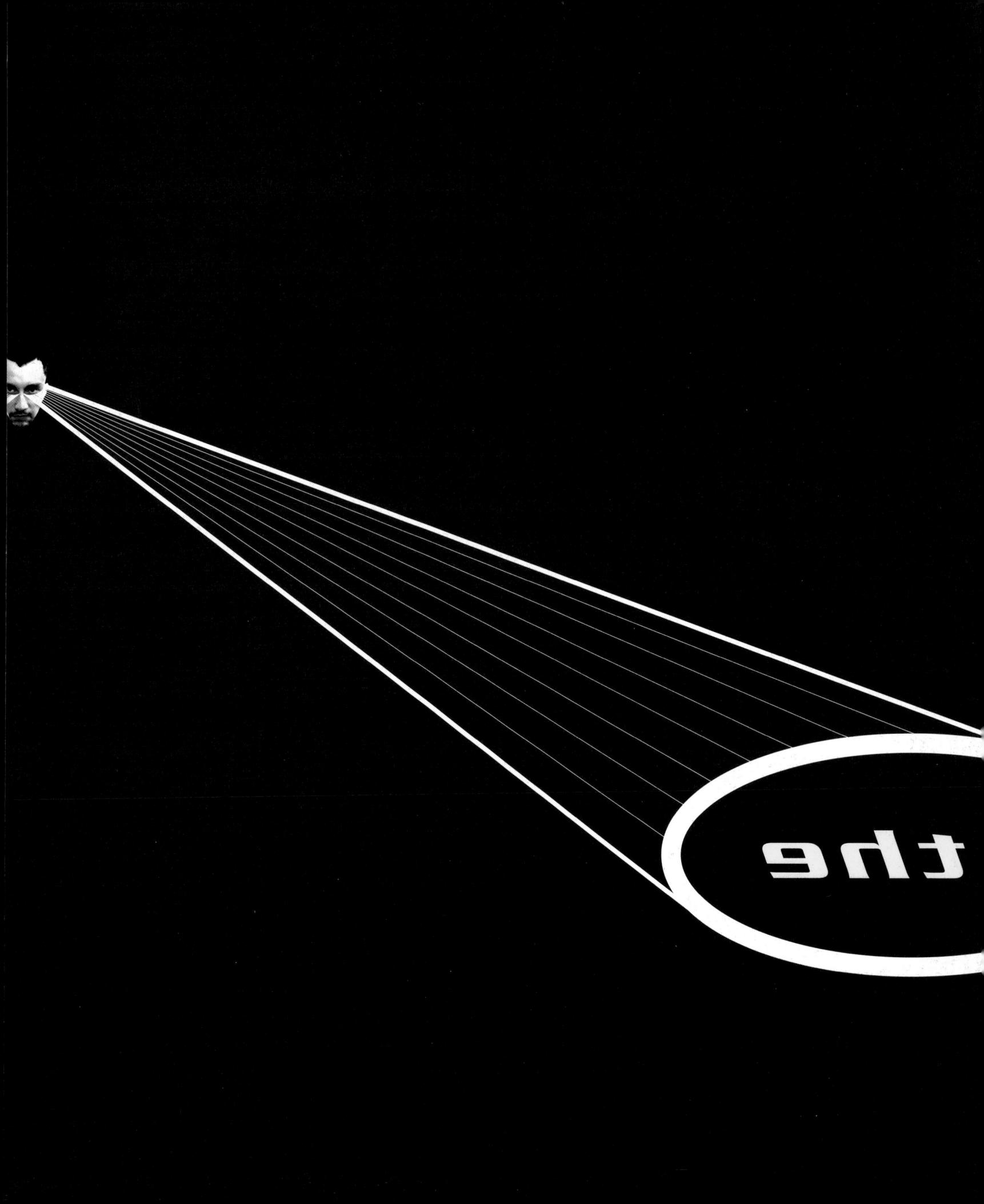

king the party to the extreme is a way to describe German raves.
veral days, too many sponsors, a dozen or so DJs and enough people to overthrow a small
untry all go into staging an event of this size. don't even ask for a guest list.

raveon

	lovepark	fullhouse	sylvester rave	holy christmas	
	125	**122**	**121**	**120**	
ais	cosmic trigger	hr3 clubnight	zoom	**128**	
8	**118**	**120**	**118**		

'96   '94   '93

flyer

age 132+133 Summer in the city is an open-air party held every weekend during the two and a half months of
ummer. The location was previously used to house milking cows, so constructing a summer utter made this piece fun.
age 130+131 Abi is another word for abitur, when students take the final exam and prepare for college. Mega-Abi is
e name given to the yearly event celebrating students' graduation. Being a party for students, using school-related
mbols made this series fun and loud. At the time mad cow disease was being documented in London, so I decided to
rrow some of its hype.

Œ ;. ˙ ˙c ˙˙˙d !"#§%&'()*+, ./++mega abi:; "="?@ABCDEFG
MJKLMNOPQRSTUVWXYZ[] _`abe ˙˙˙ ˙˙˙fghijklmn ˙˙˙˙˙Root Entry ˙˙˙˙˙˙˙˙
FÜÛ,g" ÄCompObj˙˙˙˙˙ locationideas ˙˙˙˙ B─ObjectPool

'95

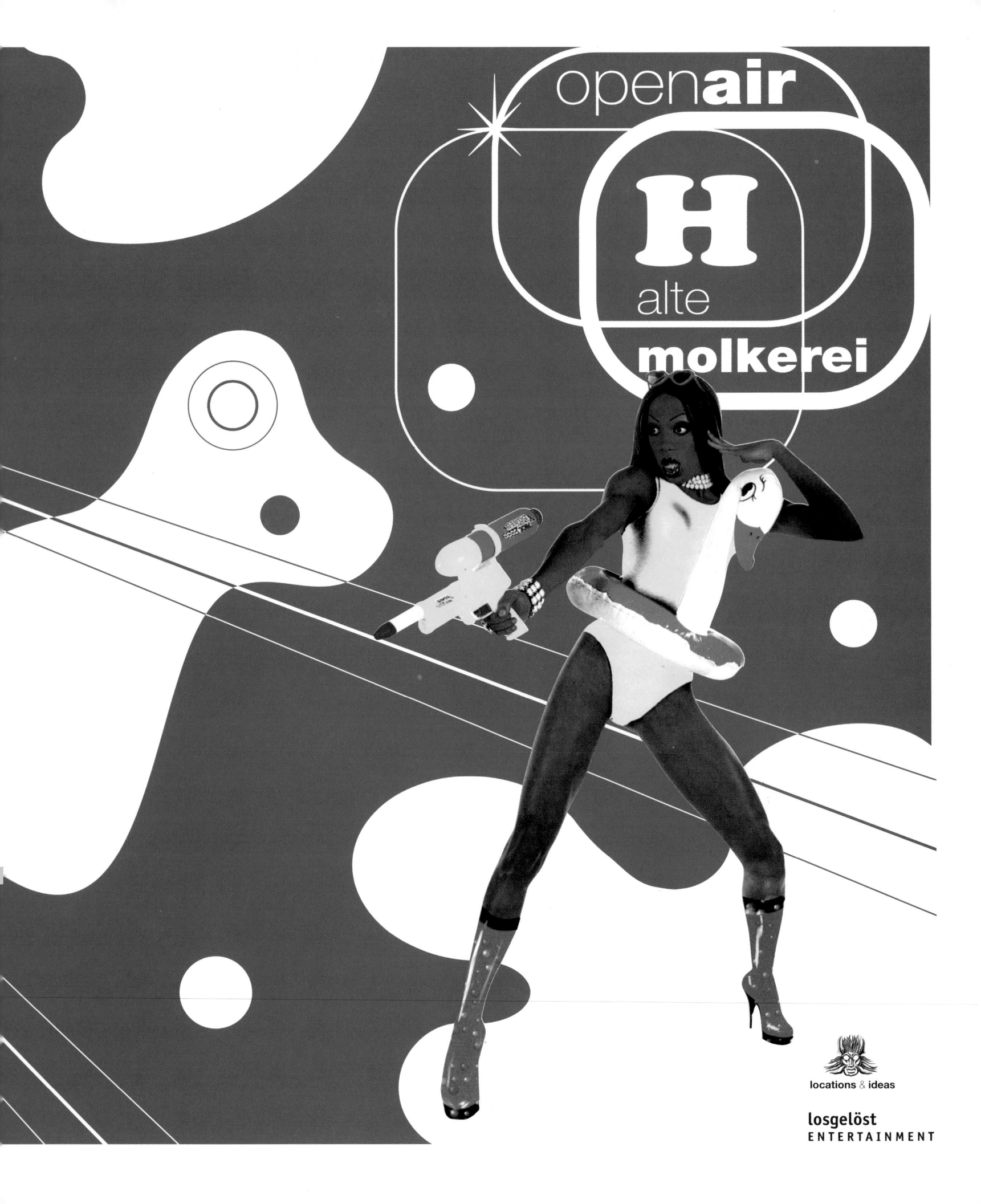

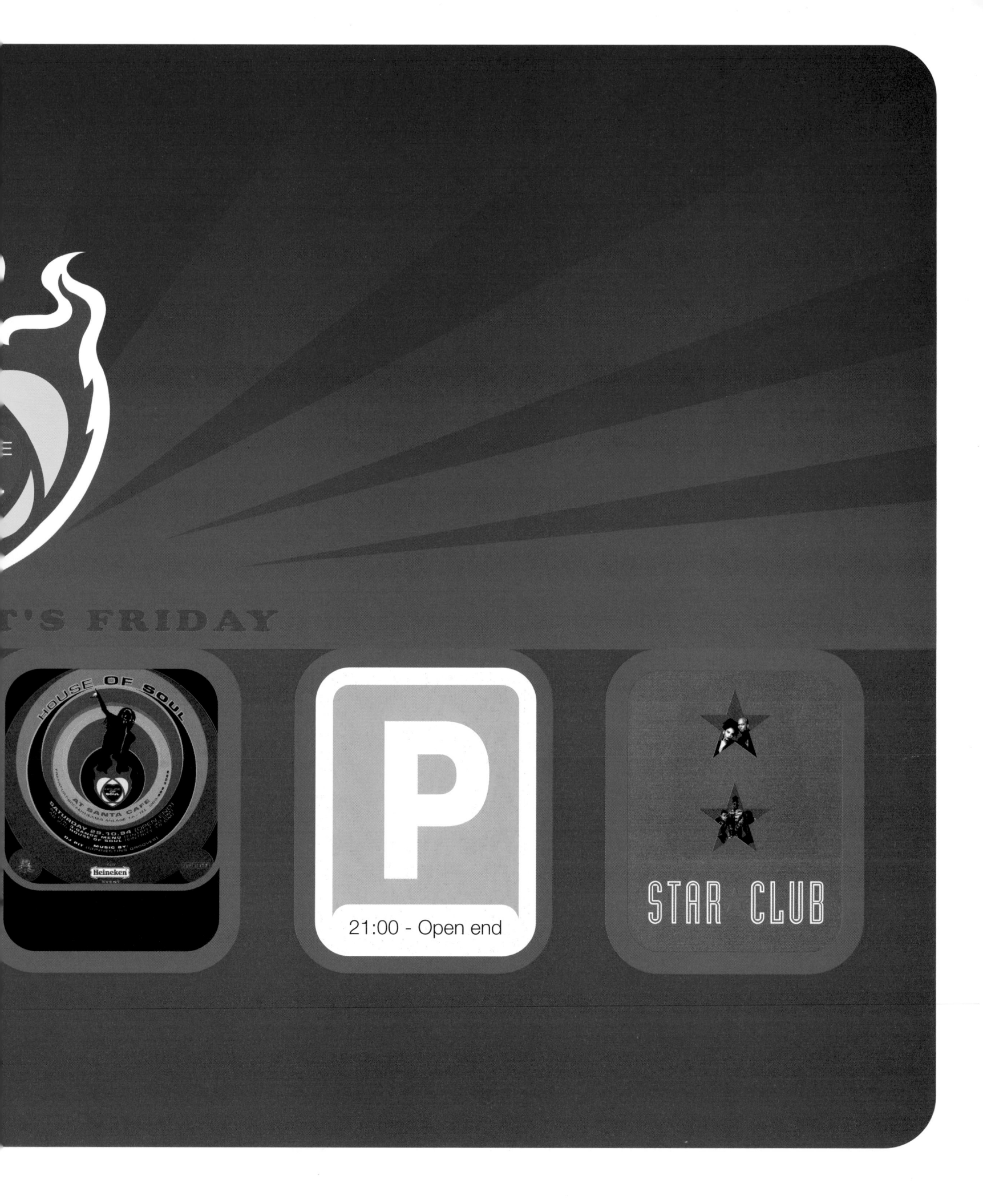

T'S FRIDAY

21:00 - Open end

STAR CLUB

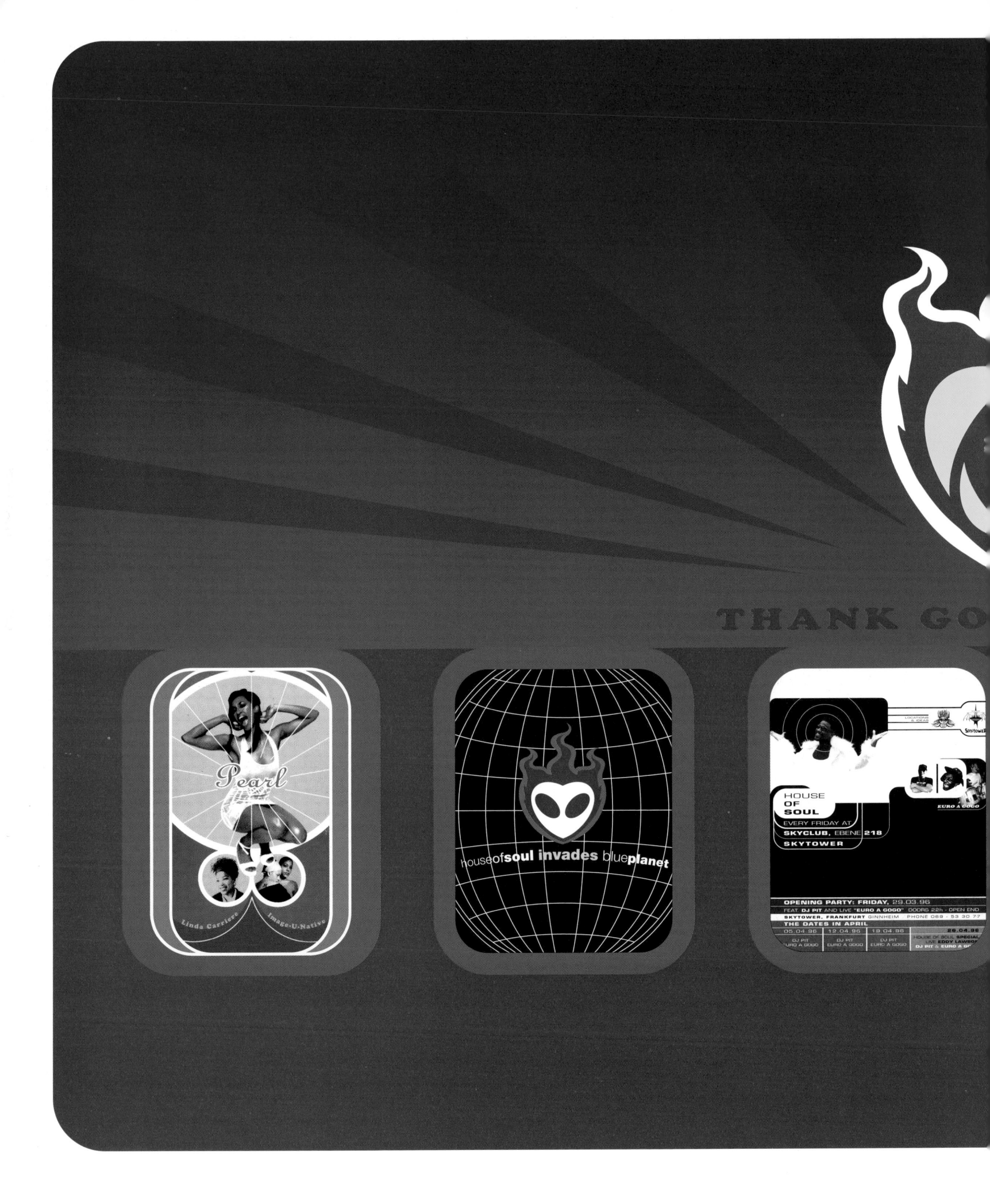

THANK GO

Pearl

Linda Carriere   Image-U-Native

houseof**soul** invades blue**planet**

HOUSE
OF
SOUL
EVERY FRIDAY AT
SKYCLUB, EBENE **218**
SKYTOWER

EURO A GOGO

OPENING PARTY: FRIDAY, 29.03.96
FEAT. **DJ PIT** AND LIVE **"EURO A GOGO"** DOORS 22h - OPEN END
SKYTOWER, FRANKFURT GINNHEIM   PHONE 069 - 53 30 77
THE DATES IN APRIL

05.04.96	12.04.96	19.04.96	26.04.96
DJ PIT EURO A GOGO	DJ PIT EURO A GOGO	DJ PIT EURO A GOGO	HOUSE OF SOUL SPECIAL w/ **EDDY LAWROC** **DJ PIT** & EURO A GO

tion&ideas

reulich, the core of the group, throw events ranging from small house
arties to mega city raves and they know the power of a good invite.

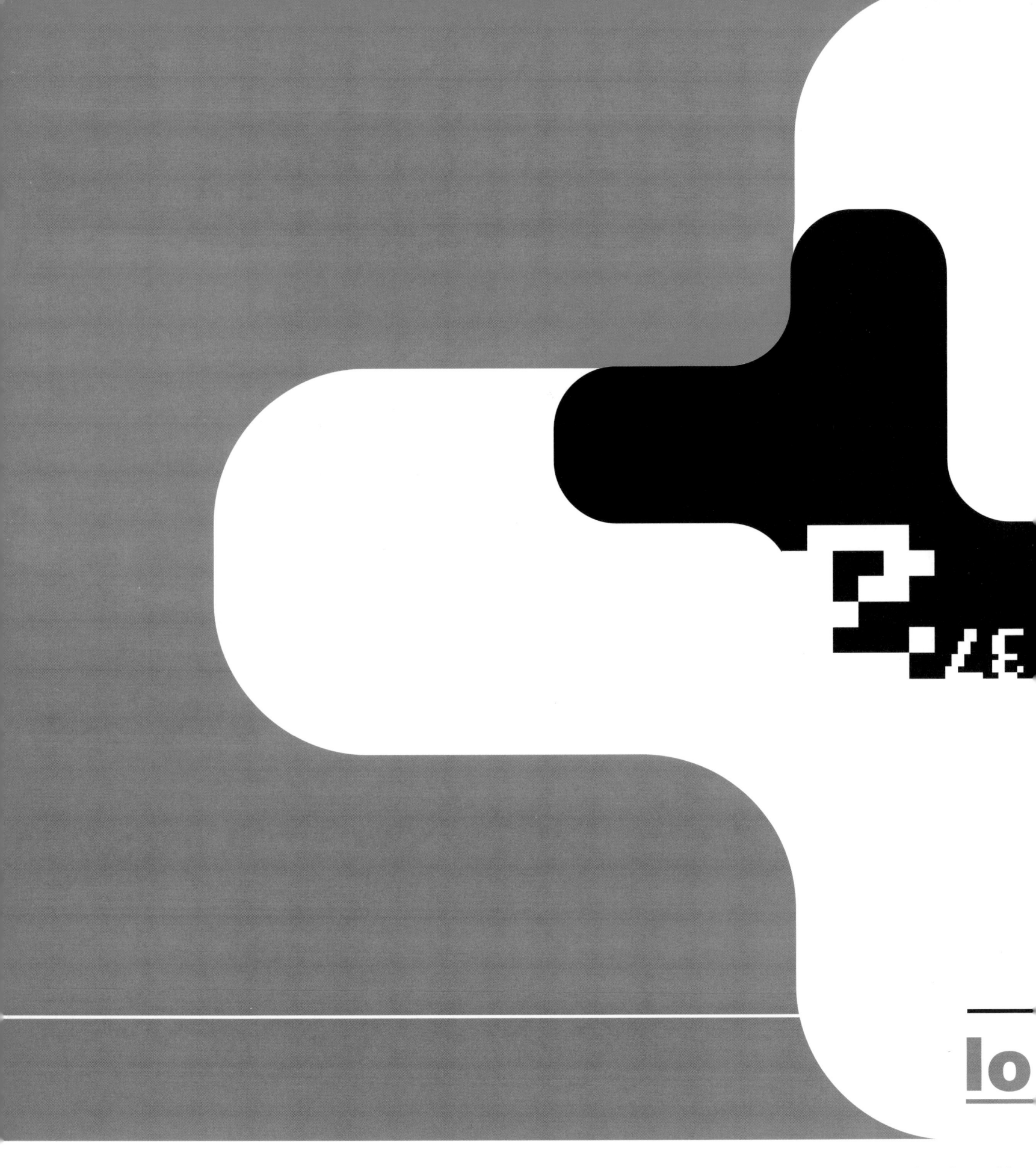

lo

whether you want to throw a party or rave you are going to need an idea and a location
but to make an event it's better to call "location & ideas". inge klausner and miche

0 bpm

SUPPORT DJ**T.** LIVE: **BANDULU**

SATURDAY 9:8:97

resistance d.00:30 **westbam**3:15

carl**cox**05:30 **talla2xlc**07:45

LOCATION: BERLINER STRASSE **60311** FRANKFURT
TELEFONISCHER KARTENSERVICE **069 - 944 36 60**

hr3
hier spielt die musik.

MTV
MUSIC TELEVISION

PRINZ
präsentiert

A PROJECT OF **1200 BPM VERANSTALTUNGS** GMBH

8.- 10. AUGUST '97

Kultura Heil Eislochs · Licher ICE BEER · epidrome

LIVEPERFORMANCE **TUNNEL**INSTALLATION **VIDEO**BEAMS

FRIDAY 8:8:97 23h SVEN**VÄTH**

dj**hooligan** 20h

SATURDAY 9:8:97

robert**miles** 22:15

mark**spoon** 01:00

12

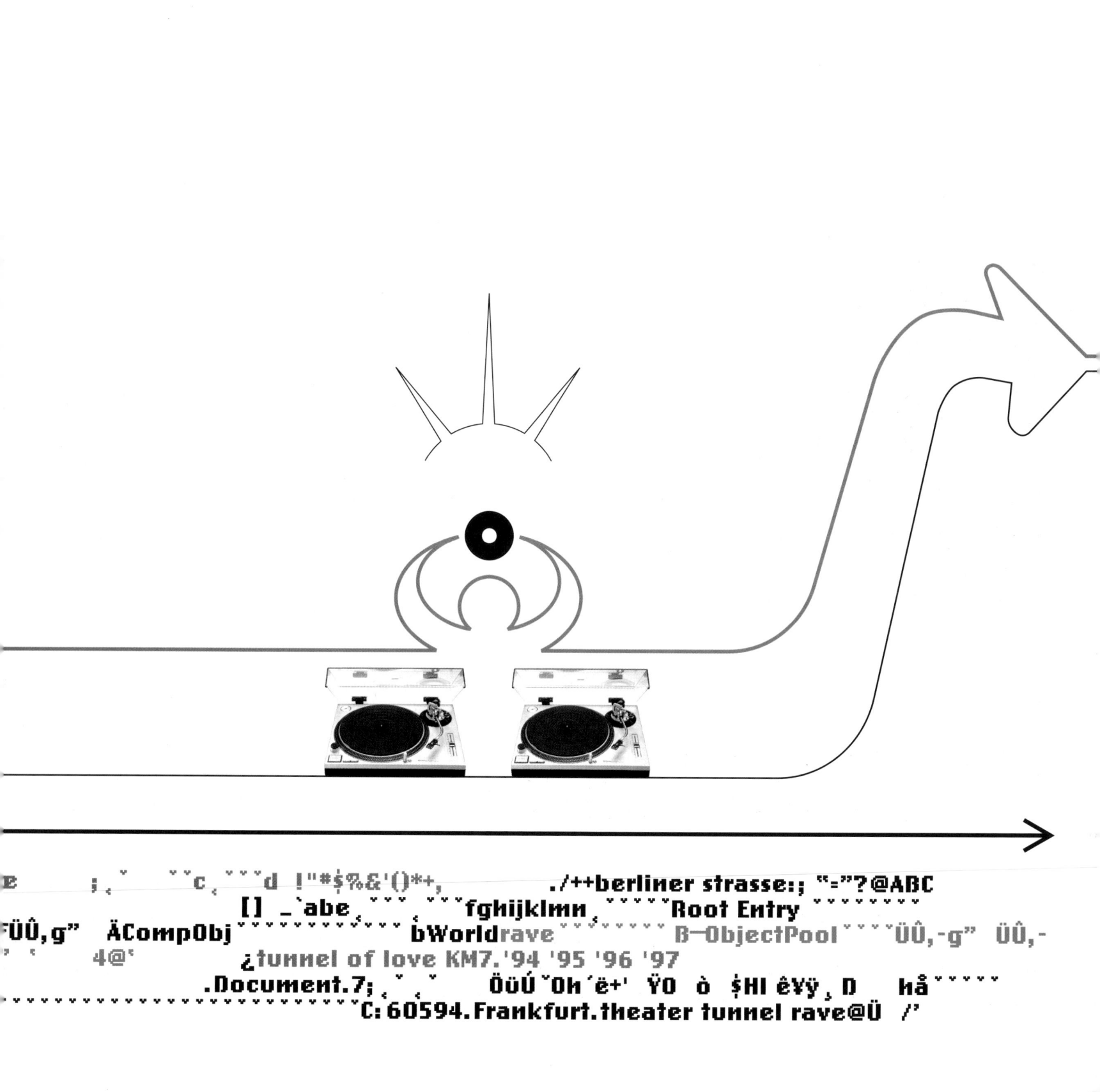

e   ;¸ ˘   ˘˘c¸ ˘˘˘d !"#$%&'()*+,   ./++berliner strasse:¸ "="?@ABC
                [] _`abe¸ ˘˘˘ ¸ ˘˘˘fghijklmn¸ ˘˘˘˘˘Root Entry ˘˘˘˘˘˘˘˘
˘ÜÛ,g"   ÄCompObj ˘˘˘˘˘˘˘˘˘   bWorldrave ˘˘˘˘˘˘   B—ObjectPool ˘˘˘˘ÜÛ,-g" ÜÛ,-
˘ ˘ ˘   4@˘   ¿tunnel of love KM7.'94 '95 '96 '97
˘ ˘ ˘ .Document.7;¸ ˘ ¸ ˘   ÖüÚ˘˘Oh´ë+' ŸO ò $HI êVÿ¸ D   hå˘˘˘˘˘
˘˘˘˘˘˘˘˘˘˘˘˘˘˘˘˘˘˘˘˘˘˘˘˘˘˘˘˘˘˘   C:60594.Frankfurt.theater tunnel rave@Ü /'

Underground was the simplest and most straightforward element of this event so I used it as the base my design. The clouds and sky images became an ongoing theme for all three events. Once the nam "Tunnel of Love" was introduced, changing established shapes into that of a heart seemed like a natu progression. At the time of the first rave DJs throughout Europe, and more importantly Germany, we being regarded as popstars, so adding their headshots probably made for a better attendance.

unnelrave 94-97

; ` ``c , ```d !"#$%&'()*+,   ./++49-69-96 21 81-30:; "="?@ABCDEFG
rliner strasse[] _`abe , ` , ` , ``frankfurt , ```` Root Entry ``````   ¿FÜÛ,g"
mpObj`````````techno Document ````````` B—ObjectPool ```¨ÜÛ,-

at do you get when you mix an abandoned subway tunnel, a thousand raving

ers and some of Europe's best DJs? A party of course. Each event lasted three days and was

moted throughout Germany.

welcome

Entry`````` **Entry**``````` ¿F ÜÛ,-g>°got the space`````floor, bar and door... find a dj````` **the dee-jay our master of sound...**```**‡ÖüÚ´Oh´ë+** ò‹$HI **now** without further delay

show me the invite

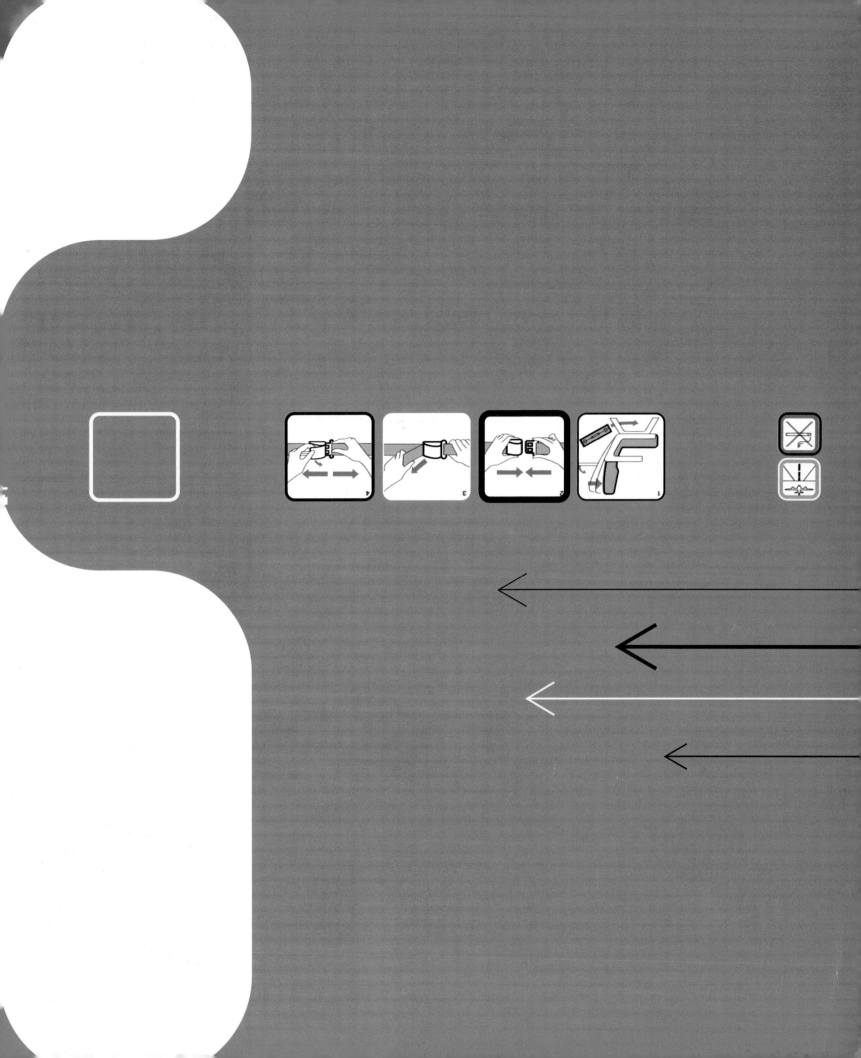

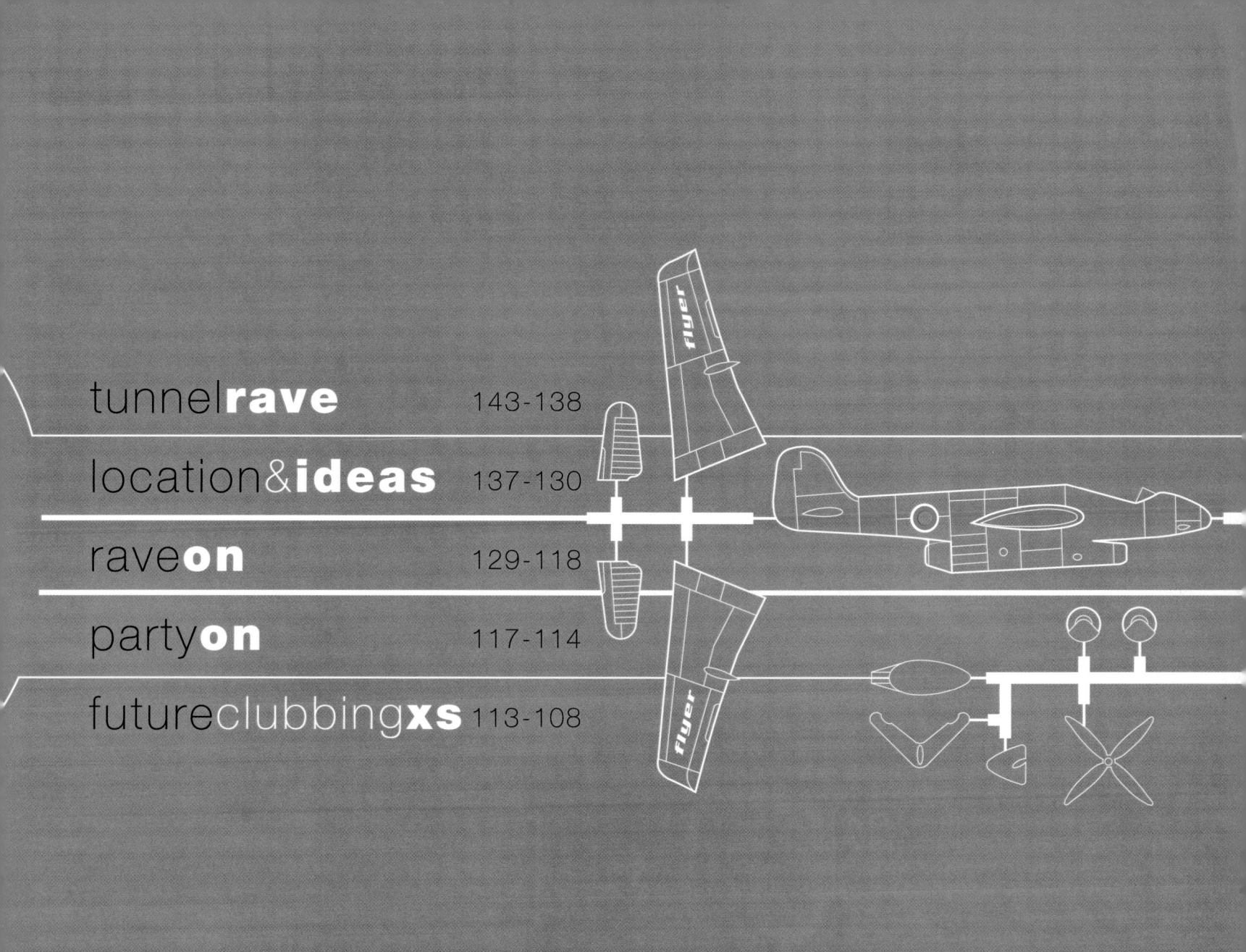

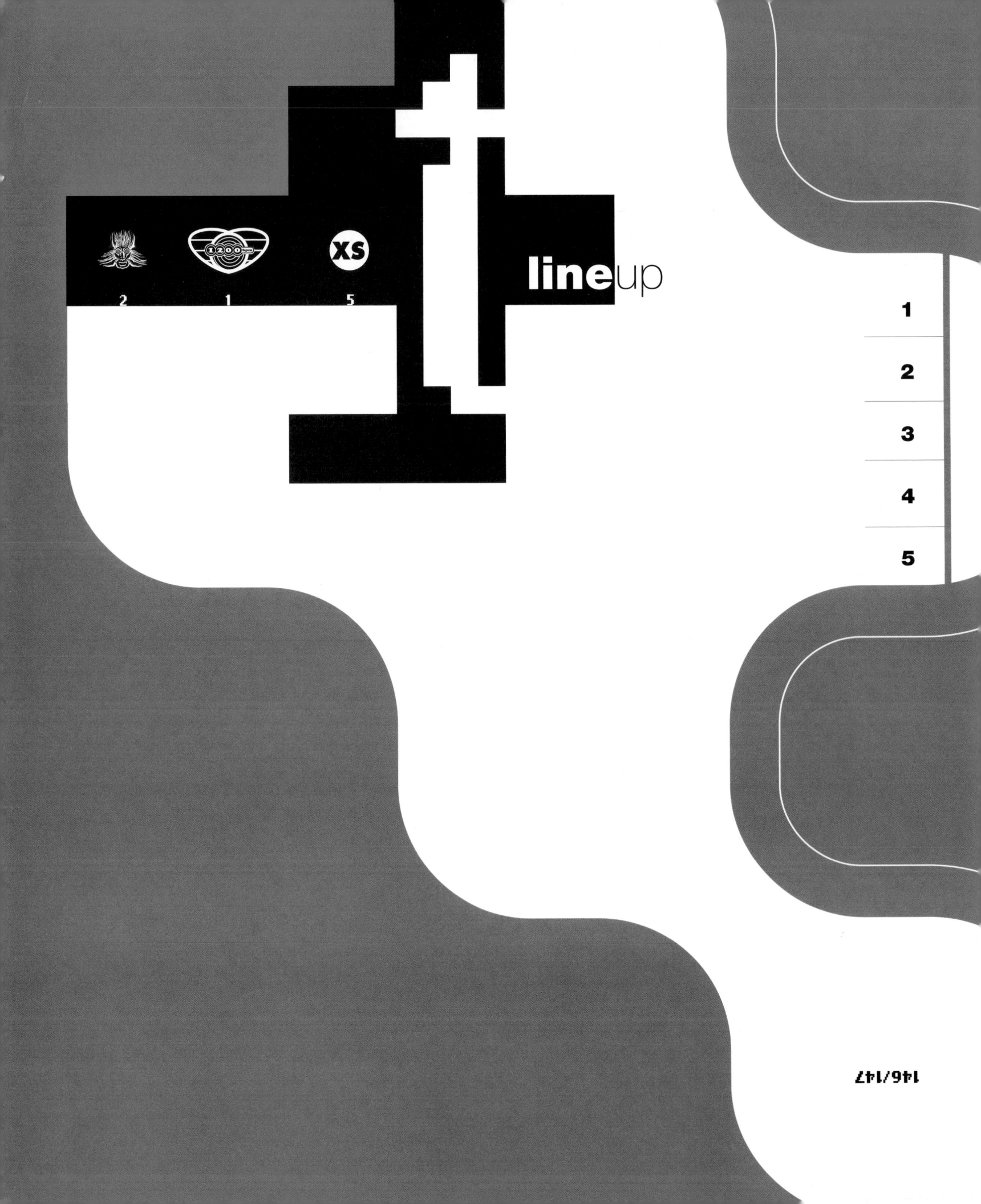

lineup

2   1   5

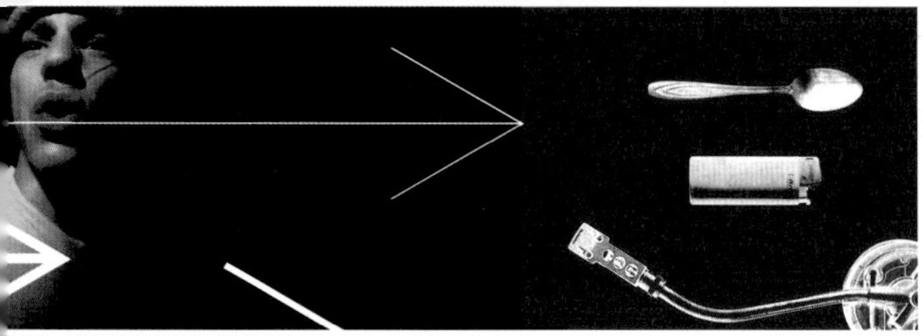

partyoverhere

..., feel the bass and taste the energy.
for those who have and have not.
where music finds its home and fashion hangs its hat.
hearts meet and bodies mingle. it's
a party, but don't forget your key, the invite.

the party started in 1992 for km7 and the doors still
haven't closed. from small get-togethers to mega raves
no event is to small for the km7 touch.
so turn up the bass and get ready to jam, there's a
party over here

Visual translator

OF DA' BASS & DA' BEAT

150

partyoverhere

ffwd